D1093687

KEY MONUMENTS
OF THE HISTORY OF ART

KEY

OF THE

OF

MONUMENTS

HISTORY

ART, *A VISUAL SURVEY*

Edited by H. W. JANSON

PROFESSOR OF FINE ARTS, NEW YORK UNIVERSITY

with DORA JANE JANSON

TEXT EDITION

PRENTICE-HALL, INC., Englewood Cliffs, N.J.

AND

HARRY N. ABRAMS, INC., New York

6730

PREFACE

THE SOMEWHAT immodest title of this volume should be understood less as an exact description of the contents than as an ideal aim which by its very nature can be realized only imperfectly. It may also serve to distinguish the purpose of the present book from that of other visual anthologies, especially those following the pattern of André Malraux's "museum without walls." Historic significance, rather than aesthetic appeal to modern sensibility, has been the determining factor in the choice of the works of art—and the photographs—here reproduced. Although the plates do not discourage the leisurely browser, they are intended primarily for a more disciplined and systematic perusal in conjunction with an introductory lecture course or with one of the numerous available one-volume surveys of the history of art. Such books do, of course, have illustrations of their own; but these are likely to be too small in size or number to provide an adequate visual documentation of the text. The lantern slides used in lecture courses are not, as a rule, subject to such limitations; on the other hand, the audience cannot study them at leisure. After remaining on the screen for a minute or two, the slides disappear and few of them are honored by a return engagement in the same course.

Key Monuments is designed to fill this gap by providing a basic stock of large, well-printed reproductions independent of (but, I trust, compatible with) any current interpretation of the history of art. Nevertheless, the selection has not been a completely impersonal, "objective" process; there is no statistical magic by which a Key Monument can be identified without fail. How, then, did I arrive at this particular choice? My starting point was a hypothetical situation: supposing that twenty leading art historians had drawn up independent lists of about 1,000 works of art for a volume such as this, on which items would they be likely to agree? The great classics, obviously—monuments such as the Parthenon and its sculpture, Chartres Cathedral, the Sistine Ceiling. By tabulating these, and checking them against the judgment of friends and colleagues, I obtained a "core list" of some 300 Monuments, not all of them necessarily of the same artistic rank, owing to the accidents of preservation, but all equally indispensable to the art historian of today. A hundred years ago—even a few decades ago—this core of acknowledged classics would have looked different in a good many significant ways; it would probably have included some artists now regarded as secondary, such as Thorvaldsen, whereas El Greco and Piero della Francesca would have been absent. These gradual shifts of art historical perspective are subtly but inescapably linked with the changing taste of every period. They affect some works of art more strongly than others, yet no work of art is wholly immune to them— there is no such thing as a perennial classic. On the other hand, the dethroned favorites of yesteryear still hold some important lessons for us, however catastrophic their fall, and I have included a number of them here (e.g., the *Apollo Belvedere* and the *Laocoön Group*) because of their tremendous impact on the taste of our forefathers.

But the agreed-upon classics do not, by themselves, constitute the history of art. As peak achievements, they are comparatively few and far between. Were we to disregard the intervening territory we should lose all sense of continuity. In these areas the historian is faced with a vastly greater number of works to choose from, and his preferences will depend on which route he takes in moving from one peak to the next. Thus the chances of agreement among the experts are correspondingly smaller, but since the individual monument does not carry quite the same burden of singularity, it is often possible to substitute one example for another of a similar kind without too painful an adjustment. About one half of my Key Monuments fall into this category. Here I have had to rely on my own judgment to a large extent, yet without a sense of departing very far from what others would have chosen in my stead.

There is still a third group of Monuments, smaller than either of those mentioned above, where the current state of scholarship did not afford me as much guidance as I needed. Some fields of our discipline are less well mapped than others, nor can I claim to read all the maps equally well. In any event, there are a number of plates (perhaps between 100 and 150) whose inclusion is in the nature of a minority report. I can only hope that they will not be felt to upset the general balance of emphasis within the volume.

Those especially interested in drawing, the graphic arts, and the applied arts (or decorative arts, or arts of design, whichever term they prefer) may be disappointed to find them largely omitted from these pages. Here I can only plead that I had to make a virtue of necessity. An attempt to illustrate the development of furniture, textiles, and ceramics—to mention only three branches of this vastly ramified subject—along with that of architecture, sculpture, and painting in a book limited to 1,000 plates, would have done less than minimal justice to any of them, and the result could have been no more than an arbitrary sampling. I thus had to impose severe limitations on my choice, based not on criteria of technique or function (which can be irrelevant and misleading) but on the individual significance and creative originality of the borderline cases.

Among the many individuals and institutions whose expert advice has aided me in selecting the Monuments and in obtaining the photographs reproduced here, I should like to thank especially the following: the late Alfred Salmony; Alfred H. Barr, Jr.; Peter H. von Blanckenhagen; Gordon Ekholm; Enriqueta Frankfort; Alison Frantz; Robert Goldwater; René d'Harnoncourt; John Pope-Hennessy; Henry-Russell Hitchcock; Pál Kelemen; Clarence Kennedy; Richard Krautheimer; Peter Murray; George E. Mylonas; Ernest Nash; Mutsumi Okada; Robert T. Paine, Jr.; Laurence Sickman; Alexander Soper; Paul Underwood; the Courtauld and Warburg Institutes, University of London; the Fogg Art Museum, Harvard University, Cambridge, Massachusetts; the German Archeological Institutes in Rome, Athens, and Berlin-Dahlem; the Oriental Institute, University of Chicago; and the Zentralinstitut für Kunstgeschichte, Munich. To them, as well as to those whose generosity is acknowledged in the captions of the plates, must go a major share of the credit for whatever good qualities this book has to offer. The shortcomings rest on my own shoulders.

H. W. JANSON

CONTENTS

IV. THE RENAISSANCE

V. THE MODERN WORLD

NOTE ON THE PICTURE CAPTIONS

All paintings are in tempera, or oil on canvas, and all sculpture is stone unless otherwise noted. Measurements are not provided for objects that are inherently large (architecture, architectural sculpture, wall painting) or small (manuscript illumination, drawings, prints). The dimensions of all sculpture are given in height only unless otherwise noted. A probable error of larger than 1 per cent is indicated by "c." Photographic sources are generally cited in abbreviated form. Full names and locations may be found by consulting the list on page 1067. Where no source is cited, the photograph has been supplied by the owner or custodian of the work.

PART ONE

THE ANCIENT WORLD

LIST OF ILLUSTRATIONS

2. EGYPTIAN ART

3. ART OF THE ANCIENT NEAR EAST

4. MINOAN AND MYCENAEAN ART

5. GREEK ART

6. ETRUSCAN ART

7. ROMAN ART

8. EARLY CHRISTIAN AND BYZANTINE ART

THE ANCIENT WORLD

1. Prehistoric and Primitive Art

Dolmen (Bronze Age Tomb). c. 1500 B.C.
Carnac, Brittany. P: ARCH. PHOT.

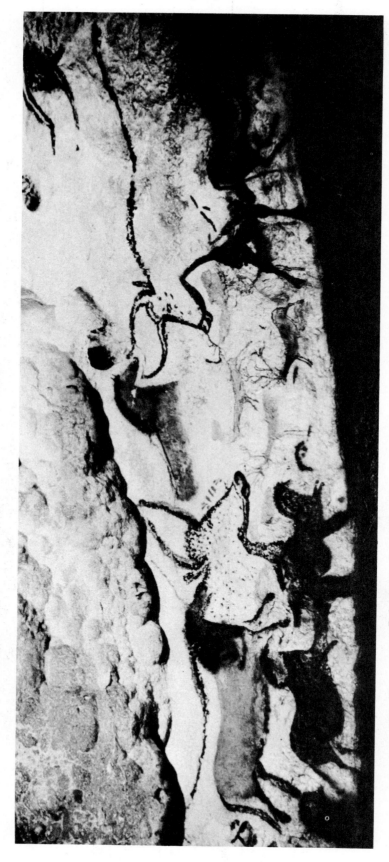

Paleolithic Cave Paintings. C. 30,000–10,000 B.C. Lascaux (Dordogne).
P: COURTESY WILLIAM CHAPMAN, FROM THE COLOR FILM *Lascaux: Cradle of Man's Art*

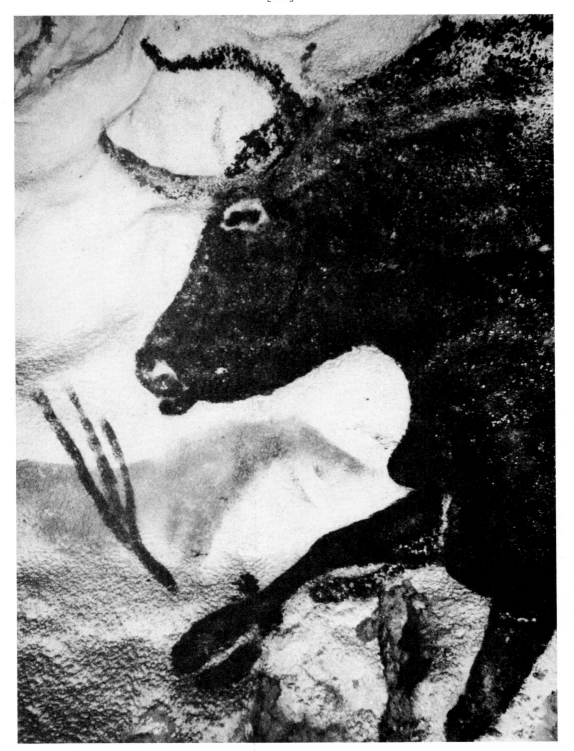

Black Bull (detail of cave painting). Lascaux. P: ARCH. PHOT.

(A) *Horse and Arrows* (cave painting). Lascaux. P: ARCH. PHOT.

(B) *Nude Woman* (carving). c. 30,000–10,000 B.C. Lifesize.
La Magdeleine Cave, Penne (Tarn). P: YAN, TOULOUSE

(A) *Wounded Bison* (cave painting). C. 30,000–10,000 B.C.
Altamira, Spain. P: COURTESY HERBERT KÜHN, MAINZ

(B) *Bison* (reindeer horn), from La Magdeleine near Les Eyzies (Dordogne).
C. 30,000–10,000 B.C. Museum of National Antiquities, St. Germain-en-Laye, France.
P: ARCH. PHOT.

Venus of Willendorf. C. 30,000–10,000 B.C. 4⅜″.
Museum of Natural History, Vienna. P: DTSCH. KUNSTVERL.

Stonehenge. c. 1800–1500 B.C. Diameter of circle 97', height of stones above ground 13½'. Salisbury Plain, Wiltshire, England.

P: MINISTRY OF WORKS, LONDON (CROWN COPYRIGHT)

The Gundestrup Cauldron (Celtic). 1st century B.C.?
Silver gilt, diameter 27″. National Museum of Denmark, Copenhagen

Bronze Disk (Celtic), from Ireland. 2nd century A.D. ? Diameter 10¾″.
British Museum, London. P: EDWIN SMITH

Wooden Mask, from Kippel, Lötschental, Switzerland. 19th century. 18″.
Rietberg Museum, Zurich (E.v.d. Heydt Collection)

Male Portrait Head, from Ife, Nigeria. 12th century. Bronze, 13½″.
Collection The Oni of Ife. P: ELISOFON

Flute Player (Benin), from Nigeria. Late 16th–early 18th century. Bronze, 25″.
Museum of Primitive Art, New York

Kneeling Woman (Baluba), from Belgian Congo. 19th–20th century.
Wood, 18½″. Royal Museum of the Belgian Congo, Tervueren, Belgium.

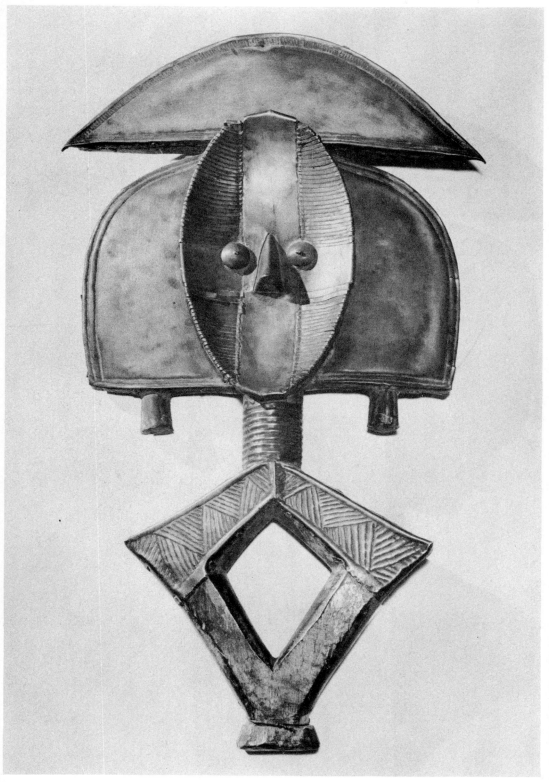

Spirit of the Dead (Bakota), from French Equatorial Africa. 19th–20th century.
Wood covered with brass, 30″. Ethnographic Collection of the University, Zurich

Mask (Bamenda), from British Cameroons. 19th–20th century. Wood, 26½″.
Rietberg Museum, Zurich (E.v.d. Heydt Collection)

Male Figure Surmounted by a Bird, from the Sepik River, New Guinea. 19th–20th century. Wood, 48″. Washington University Art Collection, St. Louis. P: SOICHI SUNAMI, NEW YORK

Mask, from the Gazelle Peninsula, New Britain. 19th–20th century.
Bark cloth, 18″. Natural History Museum, Chicago

A B O V E

(A) *Carved Lintel* (Maori), from New Zealand. 19th century.
Wood, 17½ x 36″. Peabody Museum of Salem, Massachusetts

R I G H T

(B) *Two Kangaroos*, from Oenpelli, Australia. 20th century.
Tree bark, 40¾ x 25″. Museum of Primitive Art, New York

Stone Images, on the slope of Ranu Raraku. 17th century or earlier.
Easter Island. P: AM. MUS. N. H.

Cliff Dwellings. c. 1100–1300. Mesa Verde, Colorado. P: AM. MUS. N. H.

Sand Painting Ritual for a Sick Child. Navajo, Arizona. P: AM. MUS. N. H.

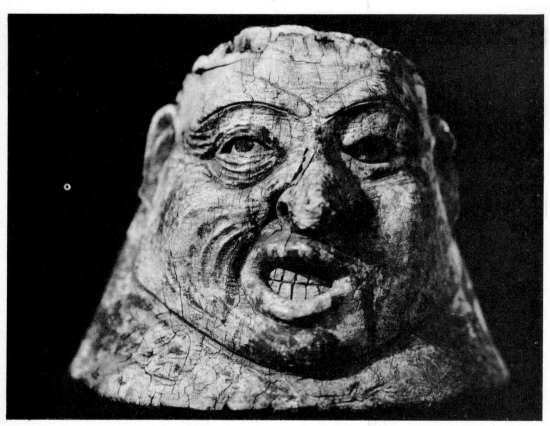

(A) *War Helmet* (Tlingit), from southeast Alaska. Early 19th century.
Wood, 12″. American Museum of Natural History, New York

(B) *Lightning Snake, Wolf, and Thunder Bird on Killer Whale* (Nootka), from Vancouver Island.
c. 1850. Wood, 68 x 118″. American Museum of Natural History, New York

Mask (representing a swan that drives white whales to the hunters),
from southwest Alaska. Early 20th century. Wood, 22″.
Museum of the American Indian, Heye Foundation, New York

Mask, from the Brakebill Mound, Tennessee. c. 1000–1600. Ocean shell, 8½ x 6½".
Peabody Museum, Harvard University, Cambridge, Massachusetts.
P: MUSEUM OF PRIMITIVE ART, NEW YORK

THE ANCIENT WORLD

2. Egyptian Art

Papyrus Half-Columns, North Palace, Funerary District of King Zoser.
3rd Dynasty, c. 2700 B.C. Saqqara. P: HIRMER

Step Pyramid of Zoser. 3rd Dynasty, c. 2700 B.C. Saqqara. P: HIRMER

(A) *The Great Sphinx.* 4th Dynasty,
c. 2650 B.C. Giza. P: HIRMER

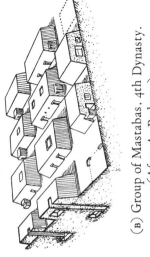

(B) Group of Mastabas. 4th Dynasty.
(After A. Badawy)

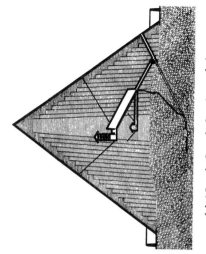

(C) North-South Section of the
Pyramid of Khufu. c. 2600 B.C.
(After L. Borchardt)

The Pyramids of Menkure (c. 2525 B.C.), Khafre (c. 2560 B.C.), and Khufu (c. 2600 B.C.). Giza. P: HIRMER

Temple of Hatshepsut.
18th Dynasty, c. 1480 B.C.
Der el-Bahri. P: HIRMER

Entrance Hall of the Chapel
of Anubis (detail of p. 47).
P: HIRMER

Three-aisled Hall of Thutmose III. c. 1470 B.C. Temple of Amen, Karnak. P: HIRMER

(B) Hall of Amenhotep III. c. 1390 B.C. Temple of Amen-Mut-Khonsu, Luxor (see "*c*" on plan). P: HIRMER

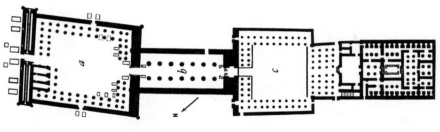

(A) Plan of the Temple of Amen-Mut-Khonsu at Luxor. (After N. de Garis Davies)

Court and Pylon of Ramses II (c. 1290 B.C.) and Colonnade of Amenhotep III (c. 1390 B.C.).
Temple of Amen-Mut-Khonsu, Luxor (see "*a*" and "*b*" on plan, page 50). P: HIRMER

Pylon and Court, Horus Temple. 237–57 B.C. Idfu. P: HIRMER

Palette of King Narmer,
from Hieraconpolis. c. 2900–2800 B.C.
Slate, 25″. Museum, Cairo.

Portrait Panel of Hesire,
from Saqqara. c. 2700 B.C.
Wood, 45″. Museum, Cairo.
P: HIRMER

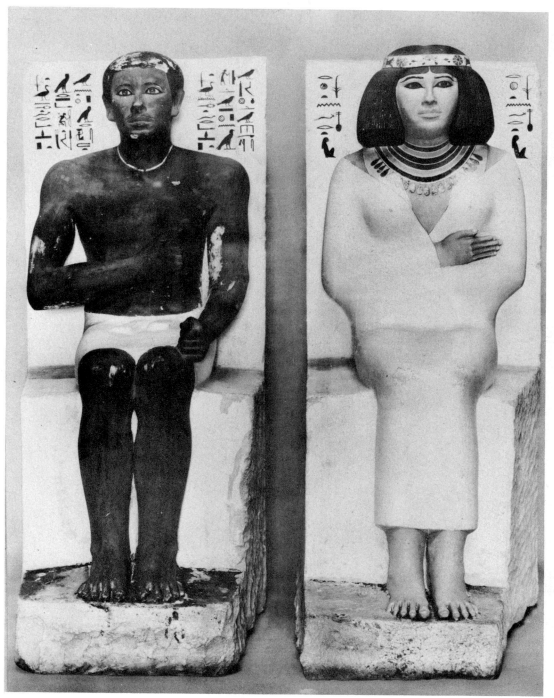

Rahotep and Nofret, from Medum. c. 2650 B.C. Painted limestone, 47″.
Museum, Cairo. P: HIRMER

Menkure and His Queen, from Giza. c. 2525 B.C. Slate, 56″.
Museum of Fine Arts, Boston

(B) *Khafre*, from Giza.
c. 2560 B.C. Diorite, 66″. Museum, Cairo

(A) *Ka-aper* ("Sheik-el-Beled"), from Saqqara.
c. 2400 B.C. Wood, 43″. Museum, Cairo

Seated Scribe, from Saqqara. c. 2400 B.C. Limestone, 21″. The Louvre, Paris

False Door and Portrait Statue of Ateti, from Saqqara. c. 2250 B.C.
Museum, Cairo. P: HIRMER

A Hunting Party on the Nile. c. 2250 B.C. Tomb of Mereruka, Saqqara. P: HIRMER

(A) *Cattle*. c. 2350 B.C. Tomb of Ti, Saqqara. P: HIRMER

(B) *King Sesostris III Represented as a Sphinx*. 12th Dynasty, c. 1850 B.C. Diorite, 16¾″.
Metropolitan Museum of Art, New York (Gift of Edward S. Harkness, 1916–17)

The Brother and Sister-in-Law of the Deceased. c. 1375 B.C.
Tomb of Ramose, Thebes. P: HIRMER

Queen Nefertiti, Sister and Wife of Ikhnaton (Amenhotep IV). c. 1360 B.C. Limestone, c. 20″.
Formerly State Museums, Berlin. P: HIRMER

(B) *Tutankhamen and His Queen* (from a throne). c. 1350 B.C.
Gold relief on wood. Museum, Cairo. P: HIRMER

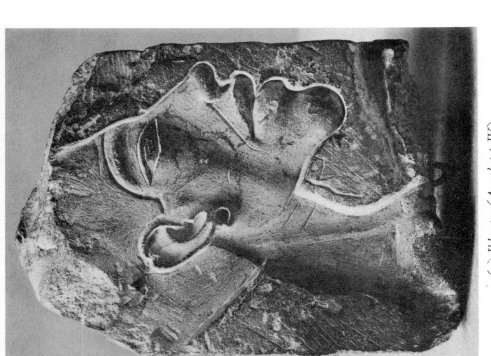

(A) *Ikhnaton (Amenhotep IV).*
c. 1360 B.C. 3⅛". Formerly State Museums, Berlin

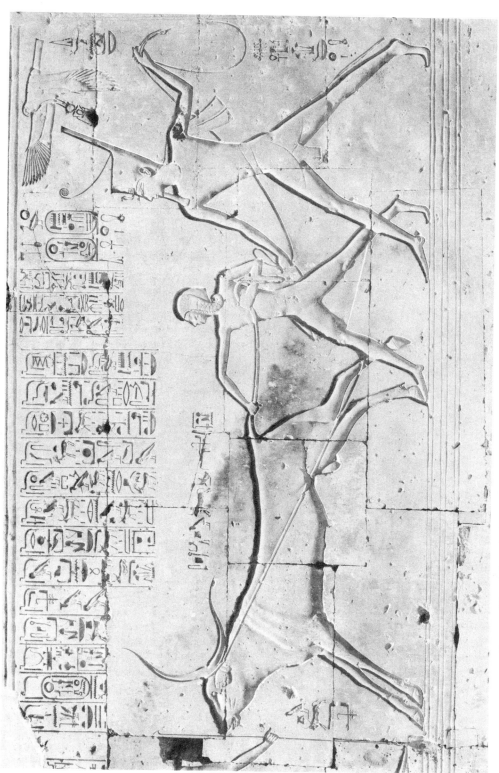

Ramses II and One of His Sons Roping a Bull. c. 1280 B.C. Temple of Seti I, Abydos. P: HIRMER

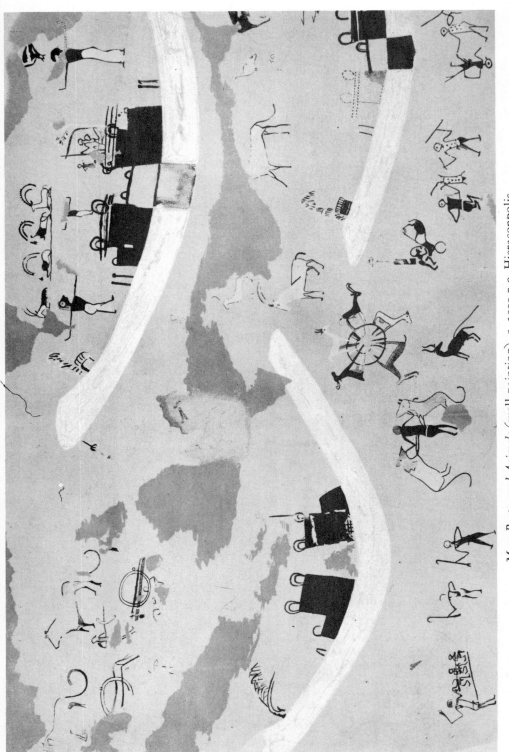

Men, Boats, and Animals (wall painting). c. 3000 B.C. Hieraconpolis.
P: FROM J. E. QUIBELL AND F. W. GREEN, *Hierakonpolis*, II, LONDON, 1902

Harvest Scenes (wall painting from a tomb). C. 1400 B.C. Thebes.

P: MET. MUS. N.Y.

(A) *Girl Dancers and Musicians* (fragment of a wall painting from a tomb), from Thebes. c. 1400 B.C. British Museum, London

(B) *The Sky Goddess Nut* (papyrus). Department of Antiquities, Cairo.
P: COURTESY TIME, INC., NEW YORK

(A) *Fowling Scene* (fragment of a wall painting), from the Tomb of Amenemheb, Thebes.
c. 1450 B.C. British Museum, London

(B) *The Daughters of Ikhnaton* (fragment of a wall painting), from Tell El-Amarna.
c. 1360 B.C. Ashmolean Museum, Oxford

(A) *A Pond in a Garden* (fragment of a wall painting from a tomb),
from Thebes. c. 1400 B.C. British Museum, London

(B) *Lion and Antelope Playing Draughts* (papyrus).
c. 1000 B.C. British Museum, London

THE ANCIENT WORLD

3. *Art of the Ancient Near East*

Head of Gudea, from Lagash (Telloh). c. 2100 B.C.
Diorite, 9″. Museum of Fine Arts, Boston

"White Temple" on Ziggurat. c. 3500–3000 B.C. Uruk (Warka). P: COURTESY GAI, BAGHDAD

Ziggurat (Elamite). C. 1250 B.C.
Dur-Untash (Chugha Zambil), Persia.
P: COURTESY THAMES & HUDSON LTD.,
LONDON, FROM S. N. KRAMER,
History Begins at Sumer

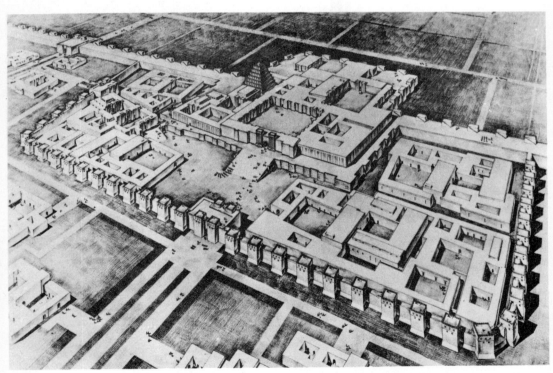

Gate of the Citadel of Sargon II. 742–706 B.C. Khorsabad,
and Reconstruction Drawing of the Citadel (by Charles Altman). P: OR. INST.

Reconstruction of the Ishtar Gate, from Babylon. c. 575 B.C.
Formerly State Museums, Berlin

The Lion Gate. c. 1400–1200 B.C. Boghazkeuy, Anatolia. P: HANS G. GÜTERBOCK, OR. INST.

Staircase to the Tripylon. c. 500 B.C. Persepolis. P: OR. INST.

Audience Hall of Darius. c. 500 B.C. Persepolis. P: OR. INST.

Achaemenian Royal Tomb. 5th century B.C. Naqsh-i-Rustam.

P: OR. INST., WITH PERMISSION OF E. F. SCHMIDT, FIELD DIRECTOR, PERSEPOLIS EXPEDITION

Palace of Shapur I. 242–272 A.D. Ctesiphon. P: OR. INST.

(B) *Sumerian Priest*, from Khafajc. c. 2500 B.C. Alabaster, 9″. University Museum, Philadelphia

(A) *Female Head*, from Uruk (Warka). c. 3500–3000 B.C. Gypsum, 8″. Museum, Baghdad. P: COURTESY GAI, BAGHDAD

Ram and Tree (offering stand), from Ur. c. 2600 B.C.
Wood, gold, and lapis lazuli, c. 20″. University Museum, Philadelphia

Bull's Head (from the soundbox of a harp), from Ur.
Wood, gold, and lapis lazuli. c. 2600 B.C. University Museum, Philadelphia

(A) Inlay on the Soundbox of a Harp,
from Ur (see p. 83)

(B) *Lilith, Goddess of Death.*
C. 2000–1800 B.C. Terracotta, 20″.
Collection Colonel Norman Colville.
P: COURTESY ENRIQUETA FRANKFORT,
THE WARBURG INSTITUTE, LONDON UNIVERSITY

Head of an Akkadian Ruler, from Niniveh (Kuyunjik).
c. 2300–2200 B.C. Bronze, 12″. Museum, Baghdad.
P: COURTESY THAMES & HUDSON LTD., LONDON, FROM
S. N. KRAMER, *History Begins at Sumer*

Victory Stele of Naram-Sin. c. 2300–2200 B.C. Stone, 78″.
The Louvre, Paris. P: EDITIONS "TEL"

Seated Gudea with Architectural Plan, from Lagash (Telloh). c. 2100 B.C.
Diorite, 29″. The Louvre, Paris. P: COURTESY THAMES & HUDSON LTD.,
LONDON, FROM S. N. KRAMER, *History Begins at Sumer*

Upper Part of a Stele with the Law Code of Hammurabi (showing the King
before the Sun God). c. 1775 B.C. Diorite, height of stele c. 7′, height of relief 28″.
The Louvre, Paris. P: EDITIONS "TEL"

The Sack of the City of Hamaan by Ashurbanipal, from Nineveh (Kuyunjik).
c. 650 B.C. 36 x 24½″. British Museum, London. P: MANSELL

Ashurnasirpal II Killing Lions, from Nimrud. c. 850 B.C.
39 x 100". British Museum, London. P: MANSELL

Dying Lioness, from Nineveh (Kuyunjik). c. 650 B.C.
British Museum, London. P: EDWIN SMITH

Frieze of Archers, from an Achaemenid Palace, Susa. 5th century B.C.
Glazed tile. The Louvre, Paris. P: ARCH. PHOT.

(A) *Darius and Xerxes Giving Audience.* C. 500 B.C.
Treasury, Persepolis. P: OR. INST.

(B) *Shapur I Triumphing over the Roman Emperor Valerian.* 260–272 A.D. Naqsh-i-Rustam.
P: COURTESY THAMES & HUDSON LTD., LONDON, FROM COSTA AND LOCKHART, *Persia,* 1958

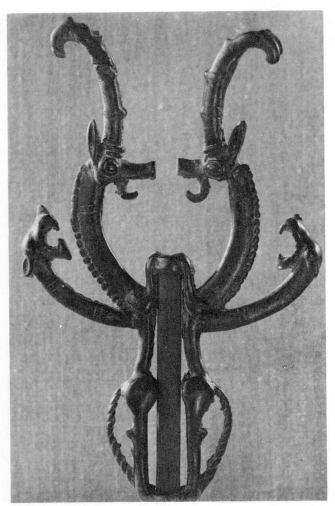

(A) *Pole Top Ornament*,
from Luristan.
9th–8th century B.C.
Bronze, 7½″.
British Museum, London.
P: EDWIN SMITH

(B) *Stag* (Scythian),
from Kostromskaya,
Southern Russia.
7th–6th century B.C.
Chased gold, c. 12″.
Hermitage Museum,
Leningrad

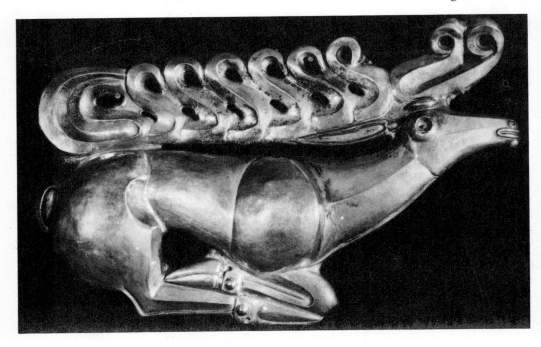

THE ANCIENT WORLD

4. *Minoan and Mycenaean Art*

The Octopus Vase (false-necked amphora), from Gournia.
c. 1500 B.C. Height 7⅝". Museum, Candia, Crete

RIGHT
The Palace of Minos.
c. 1500 B.C. Knossos, Crete.
P: FRANTZ

OPPOSITE PAGE
Stairwell, Palace of Minos.
Knossos. P: FRANTZ

The Lion Gate. c. 1250 B.C. Mycenae, Greece. P: FRANTZ

Interior and Section, "Treasury of Atreus" (Beehive tomb).
c. 1250 B.C. Mycenae. P: SBB

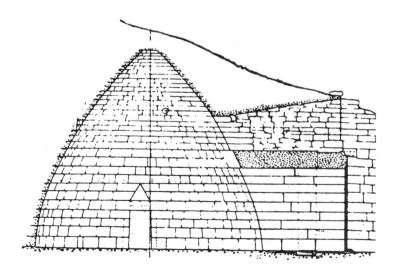

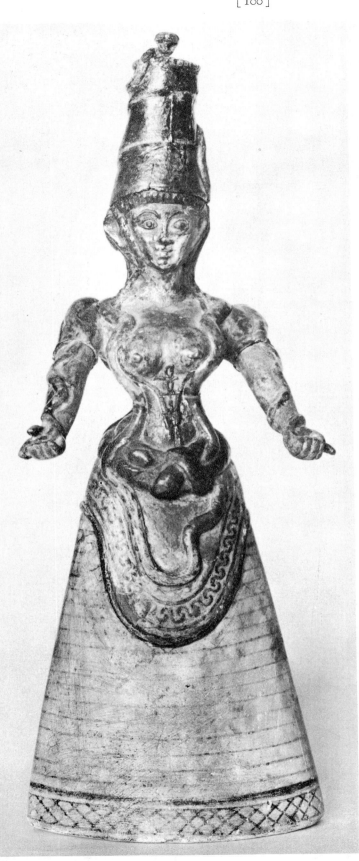

Snake Goddess (Priestess?).
c. 1600 B.C.
Terracotta, 11½".
Museum, Candia, Crete.
P: FRANTZ

Cups, from a tomb in Vaphio. c. 1500 B.C. Gold, height c. 3″.
National Museum, Athens. P: GAI, ATHENS

(A) *The Harvester Vase* (detail), from Hagia Triada. c. 1600 B.C.
Steatite, width 5½". Museum, Candia, Crete. P: FRANTZ

(B) *Painted Sarcophagus* (detail), from Hagia Triada. c. 1400 B.C.?
Height of the figures c. 8½". Museum, Candia, Crete. P: FRANTZ

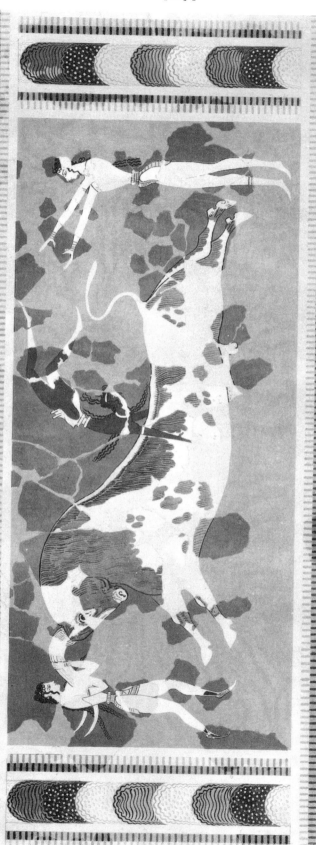

The Toreador Fresco (watercolor copy), from the Palace at Knossos. C. 1550 B.C.
Width 63″. Original in Museum, Candia, Crete. P: MET. MUS. N.Y.

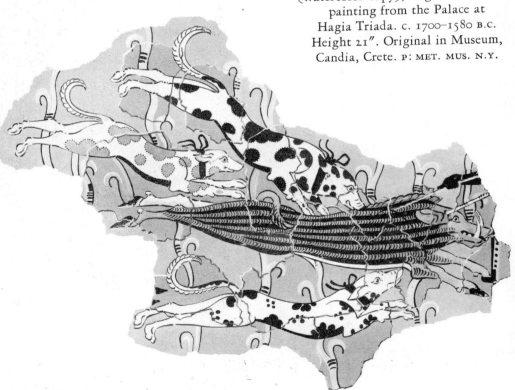

(A) *Cat Stalking a Pheasant* (watercolor copy), fragment of a wall painting from the Palace at Hagia Triada. C. 1700–1580 B.C. Height 21″. Original in Museum, Candia, Crete. P: MET. MUS. N.Y.

(B) *Boar Hunt* (watercolor copy), fragment of a wall painting from the Palace at Tiryns. 1300–1200 B.C. Width 17″. Original in National Museum, Athens. P: MET. MUS. N.Y.

THE ANCIENT WORLD

5. Greek Art

Lapith Killing a Centaur (red-figured Attic cylix). c. 490–480 B.C.
Staatliche Antikensammlungen, Munich. P: HIRMER

The "Temple of Poseidon" (c. 460 B.C.) and the "Basilica" (c. 550 B.C.).
Paestum, Italy. P: KIDDER SMITH

(B) Corner of the "Basilica." c. 550 B.C.
Paestum. P: KIDDER SMITH

(A) Interior, "Temple of Poseidon." c. 460 B.C.
Paestum. P: KIDDER SMITH

The Parthenon, by Ictinus (view from the west). 448–432 B.C. Acropolis, Athens. P: FRANTZ

Frieze on the face of the western cella wall of the Parthenon. c. 440 b.c. Acropolis, Athens. p: HIRMER

The Propylaea, by Mnesicles (view from the east). 437–432 B.C. Acropolis, Athens. P: FRANTZ

The Propylaea (view from the west) and the Temple of Athena Nike (427–424 B.C.). Acropolis, Athens. P: FRANTZ

The Acropolis in 1670 (pen drawing). Museo Civico, Bassano, Italy. P: FOND. CINI

The "Theseum" (Temple of Hephaestus). Begun 449 B.C. Athens. P: FRANTZ

The Erechtheum. Begun 421 B.C. Acropolis, Athens. P: FRANTZ

The Monument of Lysicrates.
334 B.C. Athens. P: SBB

The Theater. c. 330 B.C. Epidaurus. P: FRANTZ

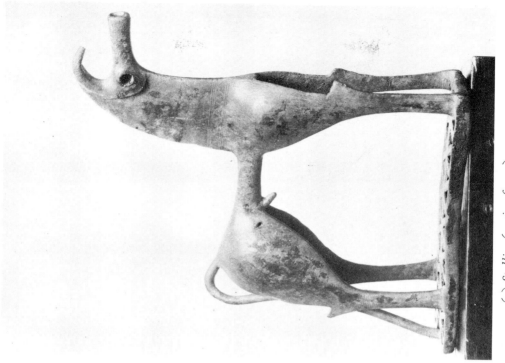

(B) *Stallion* (votive figure). C. 750–700 B.C.
Bronze, 6¼". Formerly State Museums, Berlin

(A) *Harp Player*, from Amorgos (Cyclades),
Greece. C. 2500–2000 B.C. Marble, 8½".
National Museum, Athens. P: GAI, ATHENS

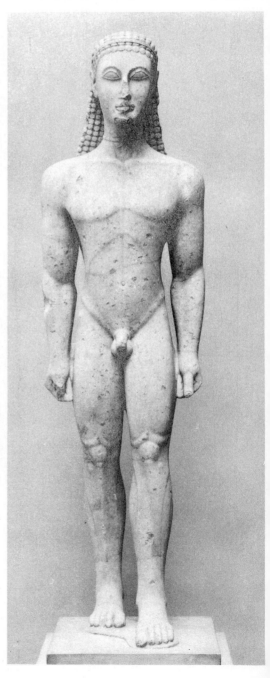

(B) *Standing Youth*. c. 600 B.C.
Marble, 73½″. Metropolitan Museum
of Art, New York (Fletcher Fund, 1932)

(A) *Female Figure*. c. 650 B.C.
Limestone, 24½″. The Louvre, Paris
(formerly Museum, Auxerre).
P: HIRMER

Calf-Bearer (upper portion). c. 570 B.C. Marble, 65″.
Acropolis Museum, Athens. P: HIRMER

Girl (Kore),
from Chios ?
C. 510 B.C.
Acropolis Museum,
Athens. P: HIRMER

The Rampin Head (from an equestrian statue?). c. 560 B.C.
Marble, 11½". The Louvre, Paris. P: HIRMER

(B) *Memorial Statue of Kroisos.*
c. 520 B.C. Marble, 76″.
National Museum, Athens.
P: HIRMER

(A) *Girl (Kore) in Dorian Peplos.*
c. 530 B.C. Marble, 48″.
Acropolis Museum, Athens.
P: HIRMER

Gorgon, from the west pediment of the Temple of Artemis, Corfu.
c. 580 B.C. Limestone, 9′ 2″. Museum, Corfu. P: GAI, ATHENS

Battle of the Gods and Giants, from the north frieze of the Treasury of the Syphnians, Delphi.
c. 530 B.C. Marble, height c. 26″. Museum, Delphi. P: HIRMER

(A) *Seated Gods*, detail
of the east frieze of
the Treasury of the
Syphnians, Delphi.
c. 530 B.C.
Marble, height c. 26″.
Museum, Delphi.
P: HIRMER

(B) Reconstruction of
the façade of the
Treasury of the Syphnians.
Museum, Delphi.
P: DR. F. STOEDTNER,
DÜSSELDORF

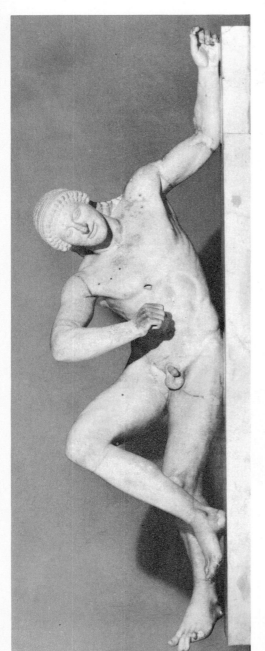

(A) *Dying Warrior*, from the west pediment of the Temple at Aegina. c. 510 B.C. Marble, 63″. Glyptothek, Munich.

P: HIRMER

(B) *Fallen Warrior*, from the east pediment of the Temple at Aegina. c. 490 B.C. Marble, 72″. Glyptothek, Munich.

P: HIRMER

Herakles, from the east pediment of the
Temple at Aegina. C. 490 B.C. Marble, 31".
Glyptothek, Munich. P: HIRMER

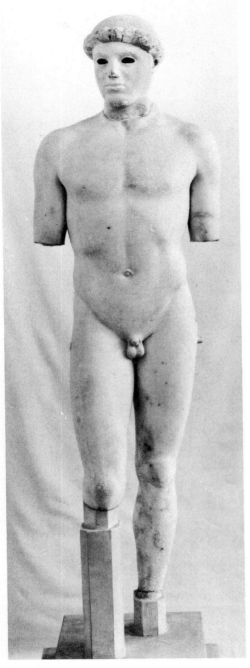

(B) *Charioteer*, from the Sanctuary of
Apollo at Delphi. C. 470 B.C. Bronze, 71".
Museum, Delphi. P: HIRMER

(A) *Standing Youth*, by Kritios?
c. 480 B.C. Marble, 34".
Acropolis Museum, Athens.
P: HIRMER

Detail of p. 128 B. P: HIRMER

Athena, Atlas, and Herakles,
metope from the Temple of Zeus at Olympia.
c. 470–460 B.C. Marble, 63 x 56″.
Museum, Olympia. P: HIRMER

Apollo (portion), from the west pediment of the Temple of Zeus at Olympia.
c. 460 B.C. Marble, over lifesize. Museum, Olympia. P: HIRMER

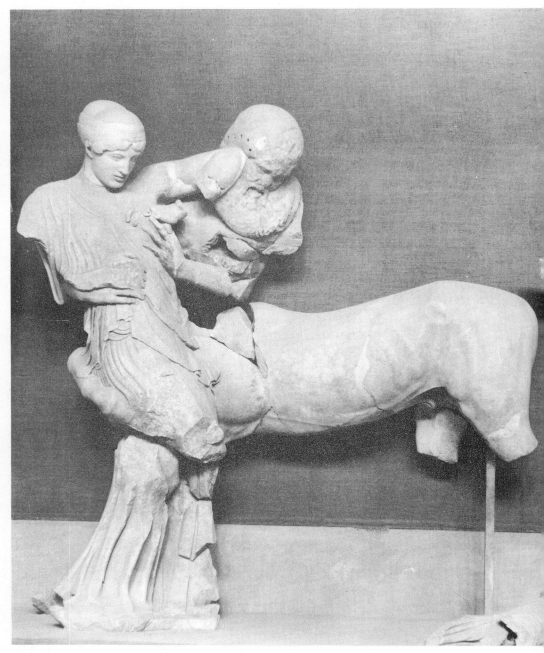

Hippodamia, the Bride of Pirithoüs, Attacked by a Centaur,
from the west pediment of the Temple of Zeus at Olympia. c. 460 B.C.
Marble, slightly over lifesize. Museum, Olympia. P: HIRMER

Poseidon (Zeus?). c. 460–450 B.C. Bronze, 82″.
National Museum, Athens. P: HIRMER

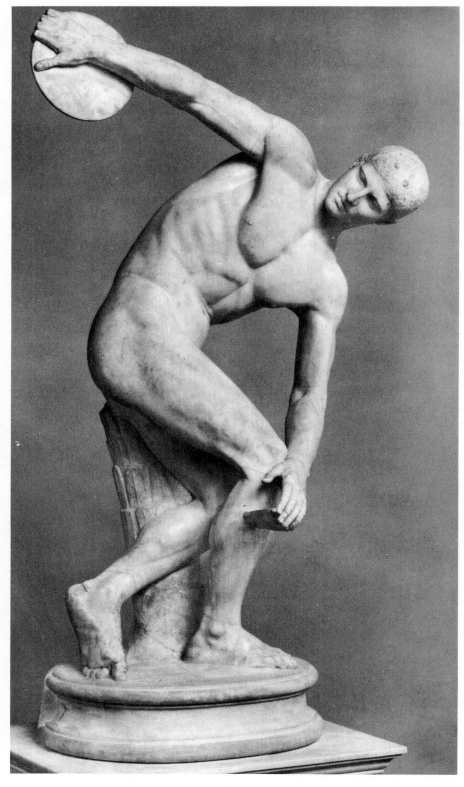

Discus Thrower (*Discobolus*). Roman marble copy after a bronze
original of c. 450 B.C. by Myron. Lifesize. Museo delle Terme, Rome

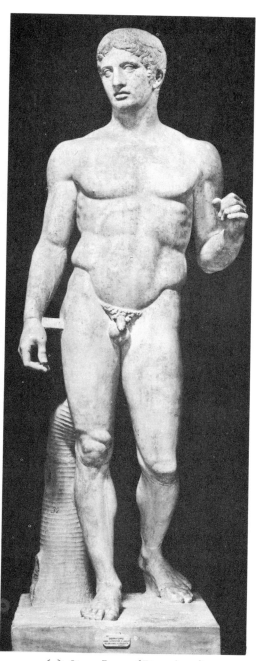

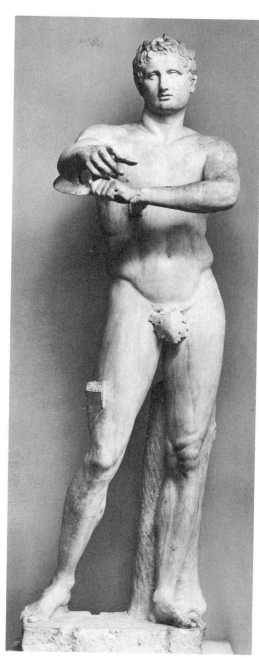

(A) *Spear Bearer* (*Doryphorus*).
Roman marble copy after an original
of c. 450–440 B.C. by Polyclitus. 78″.
National Museum, Naples.

P: ALINARI

(B) *The Scraper* (*Apoxyomenos*).
Roman marble copy after an original
of c. 330 B.C. by Lysippus.
81″. Vatican Museum, Rome

Dionysus, from the east pediment of the Parthenon. c. 438–432 B.C.
Marble, over lifesize. British Museum, London. P: HIRMER

Three Goddesses, from the east pediment of the Parthenon. c. 438–432 B.C. Marble, over lifesize. British Museum, London. P: HIRMER

Poseidon, Apollo, and Artemis, from the east frieze of the Parthenon. c. 440 B.C.
Marble, 43″. Acropolis Museum, Athens. P: HIRMER

Horsemen, from the west frieze of the Parthenon. c. 440 B.C. Marble, 43". British Museum, London. P: HIRMER

Athena Lemnia, Roman marble copy after an original of c. 450 B.C. by Phidias. Museo Civico, Bologna. P: KENNEDY

Dying Niobid. c. 450–440 B.C. Marble, 59″. Museo delle Terme, Rome. P: HIRMER

Tomb Stele of Hegeso. c. 420–410 B.C. Marble, 59″.
National Museum, Athens. P: HIRMER

Nike Taking Off Her Sandals, from the balustrade of the Temple of Athena Nike.
427–424 B.C. Marble, 42 x 20″. Acropolis Museum, Athens. P: HIRMER

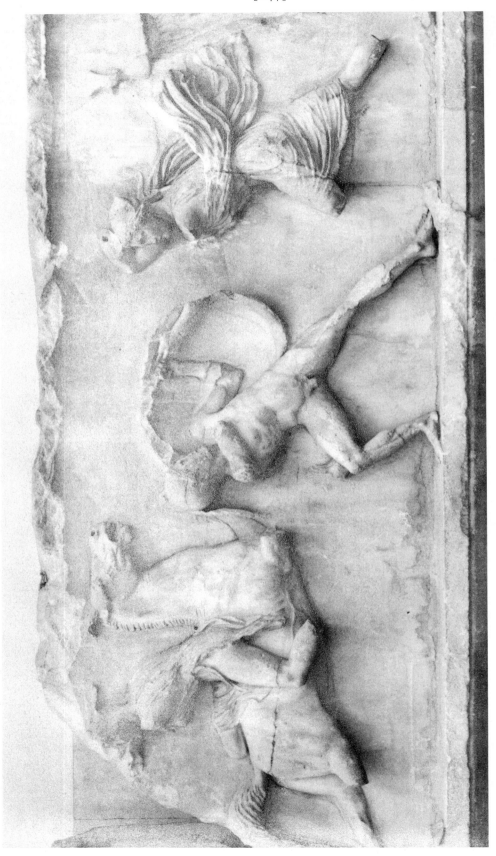

SCOPAS? *Battle of Greeks and Amazons*, from the east frieze of the Mausoleum at Halicarnassus. 359–351 B.C. Marble, 35″. British Museum, London. P: HIRMER

(A) *Mausolus*, from the
Mausoleum at Halicarnassus.
359–351 B.C. Marble, 9′ 10″.
British Museum, London.
P: HIRMER

(B) Reconstruction of
the Mausoleum at
Halicarnassus.
(After F. Krischen)

Demeter, from Cnidus. c. 340–330 B.C. Marble, 60″.
British Museum, London. P: HIRMER

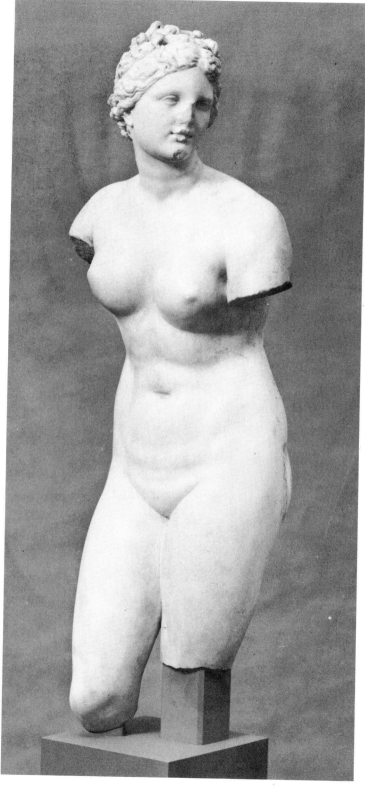

Aphrodite. Roman copy reflecting a Greek original of c. 300 B.C.
Marble, slightly less than lifesize. Metropolitan Museum of Art, New York
(Fletcher Fund, 1952)

Detail of p. 148. P: HIRMER

OPPOSITE PAGE

PRAXITELES. *Hermes.* C. 330–320 B.C. (or copy, late 1st century B.C. ?).
Marble, 85″. Museum, Olympia. P: HIRMER

The Apollo Belvedere. Roman marble copy of a Greek original of the
4th (or 1st?) century B.C. Marble, 88″. Vatican Museum, Rome

Gaul Killing Himself and His Wife. Roman copy after a bronze original of 230–220 B.C. from Pergamum. Marble, 83″. Museo delle Terme, Rome. P: ANDERSON

The Barberini Faun (detail). Roman copy of a Greek original of c. 220 B.C.
Marble, over lifesize. Glyptothek, Munich. P: HIRMER

Nike of Samothrace. C. 200 B.C. The Louvre, Paris. P: HIRMER

(A) *Athena and Alcyoneus*, detail of the Great Frieze of the Altar of Zeus at Pergamum.
c. 180 B.C. Marble, 90". Formerly Pergamum Museum, Berlin

(B) Reconstruction of the west front
of the Altar of Zeus at Pergamum.
Formerly Pergamum Museum, Berlin

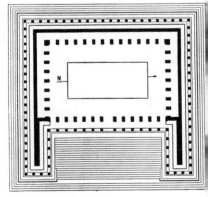

(C) Plan of the Altar of Zeus at
Pergamum. (After J. Schrammen)

AGESANDER, ATHENODORUS, and POLYDORUS OF RHODES. *The Laocoön Group.* 1st century B.C.
Marble, 95″. Vatican Museum, Rome. P: HIRMER

(B) *Thorn Puller (Spinario)*. Roman bronze (the body reflects a 4th-century Greek original), 28¾″.

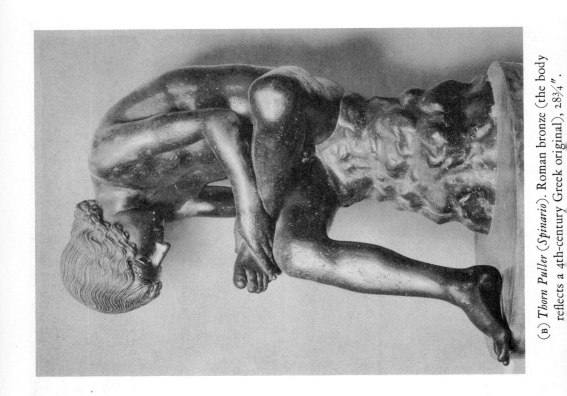

(A) *Portrait Head*, from Delos. c. 80 B.C. Bronze, 13″. National Museum, Athens. P: HIRMER

Boxer. c. 50 B.C. Bronze, 50″. Museo delle Terme, Rome. P: HIRMER

LEFT

(A) *Winged God* (silver coin),
from Peparethus, c. 500 B.C.
Diameter 1½″. P: HIRMER

BELOW

(B) *Chariot* (ten-drachma silver
coin), from Syracuse. 479 B.C.
Diameter 1½″. P: HIRMER

RIGHT

(A) *Silenus* (silver coin), from Naxos.
461 B.C. Diameter 1¼″.

P: HIRMER

BELOW

(B) *Two Eagles on a Hare* (silver
coin), from Akragas. c. 408 B.C.
Diameter 1½″. P: HIRMER

(A) *Apollo* (silver coin), from Catana. C. 415 B.C. Diameter 1⅛″.

P: HIRMER

(B) *Alexander the Great with Amon Horns* (four-drachma silver coin), issued by Lysimachus. C. 300 B.C. Diameter 1⅛″. P: HIRMER

Mourning Scene and Funeral Procession (Dipylon vase). 8th century B.C. 42½″.
Metropolitan Museum of Art, New York (Rogers Fund, 1914)

The Blinding of Polyphemus and *Gorgons* (Proto-Attic amphora). c. 675–650 B.C. 56″.
Museum, Eleusis, Greece. P: COURTESY GEORGE E. MYLONAS, ST. LOUIS

(A) Proto-Corinthian Perfume
Vase. Early 6th century B.C.
The Louvre, Paris

(B) EXEKIAS. *Dionysus in a Boat* (black-figured Attic cylix).
c. 540 B.C. Staatliche Antikensammlungen, Munich

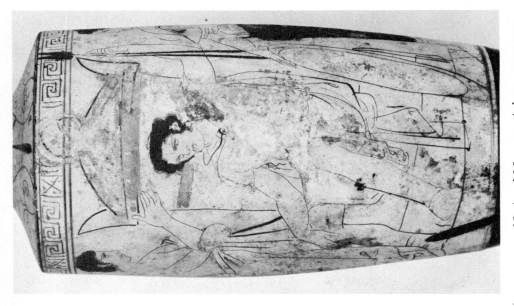

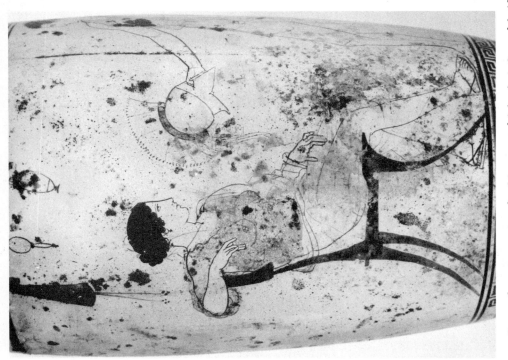

Scenes from two painted white-ground lekythoi. Second half of 5th century B.C. National Museum, Athens. P: FRANTZ

The Defeated Persians under Darius, detail of *The Battle of Issus*. Roman mosaic copy, from Pompeii, of a Greek painting of the late 4th century B.C. Width of the portion reproduced c. 10½′. National Museum, Naples. P: ALINARI

The Knuckle-Bone Players. Roman copy, from Herculaneum, reflecting a Greek original (by Alexandros of Athens?) of the late 5th century B.C. Marble panel, 16½ x 15″. National Museum, Athens. P: ALINARI

THE ANCIENT WORLD

6. Etruscan Art

Porta Augusta (Etruscan city gate). 2nd century B.C.
Perugia. P: ANDERSON

Burial Chamber, "Tomb of the Reliefs." Late 5th century B.C. Cerveteri. P: ALTEROCCA, TERNI

Reclining Couple, sarcophagus from Cerveteri. Late 6th century B.C.
Clay, 79″. Villa Giulia Museum, Rome. P: GFN

Apollo, from Veii.
c. 500 B.C. Clay, 69″.
Villa Giulia Museum,
Rome. P: GAI, ROME

Statue of an Official (*L'arringatore*). C. 150 B.C. Bronze, 71″.
Archeological Museum, Florence. P: ANDERSON

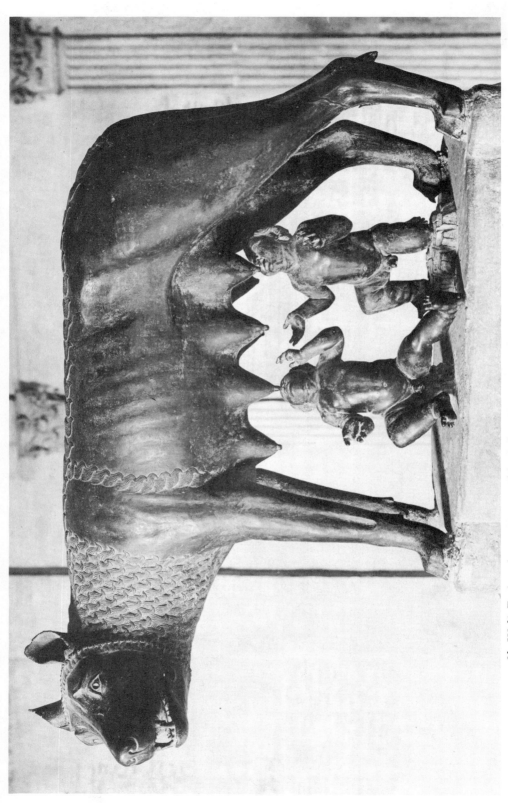

She-Wolf. Early 5th century B.C. (the infants Romulus and Remus are Renaissance additions).
Bronze, c. 52″. Capitoline Museums, Rome. P: GFN

Wall Painting (detail).

c. 520 B.C. "Tomb of Hunting and Fishing," Tarquinia. P: ANDERSON

Details of Wall Paintings in the "Tomb of the Leopards"
(c. 480 B.C.) and in the "Tomb of the Lionesses" (c. 480–470 B.C.).
Tarquinia. P: BROGI

THE ANCIENT WORLD

7. Roman Art

Gemma Augustea (Augustus and Roma witnessing
the Triumph of Tiberius, 12 A.D.). Late 1st century A.D. Oynx,
7½ x 9". Kunsthistorisches Museum, Vienna

(A) The Pantheon. c. 115/125 A.D. Rome. P: FOT. UNIONE

(B) The Colosseum (aerial view). 72–80 A.D. Rome. P: FOTOCIELO, ROME

Detail of p. 176 B. P: KIDDER SMITH

The Interior of the Pantheon, painting by Giovanni Paolo Panini. c. 1750.
50½ x 39". National Gallery of Art, Washington, D. C. (Kress Collection)

(A) Temple of the Sibyl. Early 1st century B.C. Tivoli. P: ALINARI

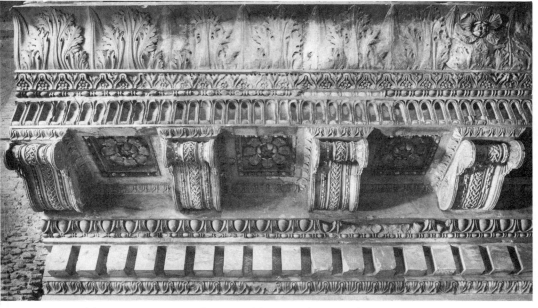

(B) Marble Cornice, from the Temple of Concord. 1st century A.D.
Tabularium, Forum Romanum, Rome. P: ANDERSON

OPPOSITE PAGE
"Maison Carrée."
Completed 16 B.C. Nîmes.
P: SCHMIDT-GLASSNER,
DTSCH. KUNSTVERL.

RIGHT
Pont du Gard (aqueduct).
Early 1st century A.D.
Nîmes. P: ROUBIER

(A) Peristyle, House of the Vettii. c. 50 A.D.
Pompeii. P: ALINARI

(B) Atrium, House of the *triclinio a mosaico*. 1st century B.C.
Herculaneum. P: ALINARI

Apartment Houses. 2nd century A.D. Ostia. P: FOT. UNIONE

Porta Nigra (city gate). Early 4th century A.D. Trier, Germany. P: SBB

Reconstruction of city gate from Miletus. c. 160 A.D. Formerly Pergamum Museum, Berlin

Cella Wall, Temple of Bacchus. 2nd century A.D.
Baalbek. P: KIDDER SMITH

Temple of Venus.
3rd century A.D. Baalbek.
P: SBB (ABOVE)
AND D. SARRAFIAN, BEIRUT

Mausoleum, Palace of Diocletian. c. 300 A.D. Split, Yugoslavia.
[Engraving by Robert Adam, *Ruins of the Palace of the Emperor Diocletian*, 1764.
Metropolitan Museum of Art, New York (Beattie Collection, 1941)]

(A) Peristyle, Palace of Diocletian. P: COURTESY YUGOSLAV STATE TOURIST OFFICE, NEW YORK

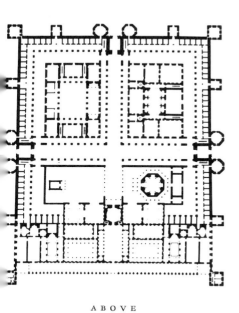

ABOVE
(B) Plan of the Palace of Diocletian
(by Robert Adam)

RIGHT
(C) East Gate, Palace of Diocletian.
P: MARBURG

Basilica. Early 3rd century A.D. Leptis Magna, North Africa. P: GAI, ROME

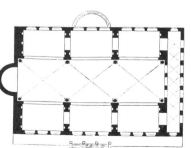

(A) Plan of the Basilica, Leptis Magna

ABOVE AND RIGHT (B, C) Plan and view of the Basilica of Constantine. c. 310–320 A.D. Rome. P: KIDDER SMITH

Reconstruction Model of the Imperial Forums of Rome. p: FOT. UNIONE

*A Roman Patrician with
Busts of His Ancestors.*
1st century A.D.
Marble, lifesize.
Barberini Palace, Rome.
P: ALINARI

Augustus of Primaporta. c. 20 B.C. Marble, 80″. Vatican Museum, Rome

Detail of p. 194

Ornament from the base of the Ara Pacis. 13–9 B.C. Marble, 72″.
Rome. P: ANDERSON

Imperial Procession, from the frieze of the Ara Pacis.
Marble, 63″. Rome. P: ANDERSON

Triumph of Titus, reliefs from the Arch of Titus. 81 A.D.
Marble, 94″. Rome. P: ALINARI

Lower portion of Trajan's Column. 106–113 A.D. Marble,
height of relief band c. 50″. Rome. P: KIDDER SMITH

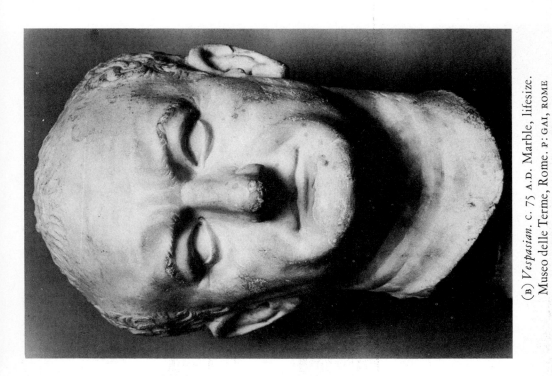

(B) *Vespasian.* C. 75 A.D. Marble, lifesize.
Museo delle Terme, Rome. P: GAI, ROME

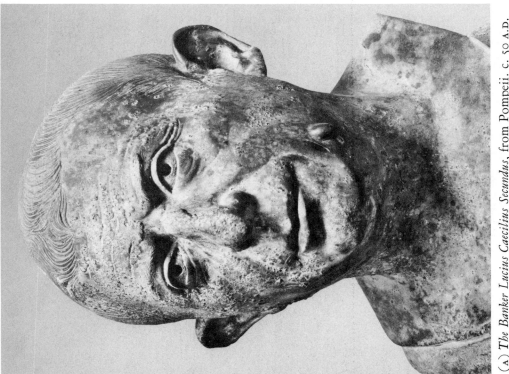

(A) *The Banker Lucius Caecilius Secundus, from Pompeii.* c. 50 A.D.
Bronze, lifesize. National Museum, Naples. P: ANDERSON

Portrait of a Lady. Late 1st century A.D. Marble, lifesize. Capitoline Museums, Rome. P: GAI, ROME

Trajan. c. 100 A.D. Marble, lifesize. Museum, Ostia

Equestrian Statue of Marcus Aurelius. 161–180 A.D. Bronze, over lifesize.
Piazza del Campidoglio, Rome (see p. 678A). P: ALINARI

Battle of Romans and Barbarians, from the *Ludovisi Sarcophagus*. 1st half of 3rd century A.D.
Marble, 98″. Museo delle Terme, Rome. P: ANDERSON

(B) *Maenad* (Neo-Attic relief). 1st century A.D. Marble, 56½ x 28″. Capitoline Museums, Rome.
P: ALINARI

(A) Stucco Decoration from the vault of a Roman House. End of 1st century B.C. Museo delle Terme, Rome. P: ANDERSON

Portrait Head (probably of the philosopher Plotinus). Late 3rd century A.D.
Marble, lifesize. Museum, Ostia. P: GFN

Colossal Head of Constantine the Great. Early 4th century A.D.
Marble, 95″. Capitoline Museums, Rome. P: HIRMER

The Arch of Constantine. Early 4th century A.D. Rome. P: ANDERSON

Medallions (of the time of Hadrian, 117–138 A.D.) and Frieze (early 4th century),
detail of the Arch of Constantine. P: ALINARI

Wall Painting. c. 50 B.C. Villa of the Mysteries, Pompeii. P: ALINARI

View of a Garden, detail of a wall painting from the Villa of Livia at Primaporta.
C. 20 B.C. Museo delle Terme, Rome. P: ANDERSON

Detail of p. 210. P: ANDERSON

Hercules and Telephus, wall painting from Herculaneum. 1st century B.C.
National Museum, Naples. P: ANDERSON

Architectural View, wall painting from a villa at Boscoreale. 1st century B.C.
Metropolitan Museum of Art, New York (Rogers Fund, 1903)

Peaches and Glass Jug, wall painting from Herculaneum. c. 50 A.D.
National Museum, Naples. P: SOPRINTENDENZA ALLE ANTICHITÀ DELLA CAMPANIA

View of a Harbor, portion of a wall painting
from Stabiae. c. 50 A.D.
National Museum, Naples. P: ANDERSON

Gladiators, detail of a mosaic pavement from a villa at Torrenuova. c. 300 A.D. Borghese Gallery, Rome. P: ANDERSON

The Ixion Room. 63–79 A.D. House of the Vettii, Pompeii. P: ALINARI

North half (portion) of the west wall of the Assembly Hall of the Synagogue at Dura-Europos. 245–256 A.D.
National Museum, Damascus. P: COURTESY DURA-EUROPOS PUBLICATIONS, YALE UNIVERSITY

Portrait of a Boy, from the Faiyum, Lower Egypt. 2nd century A.D.
Encaustic on wood, 13 x 7¼". Metropolitan Museum of Art,
New York (Gift of Edward S. Harkness, 1918)

THE ANCIENT WORLD

8. Early Christian and Byzantine Art

The Parting of Lot and Abraham (mosaic). C. 435 A.D.
S. Maria Maggiore, Rome. P: ANDERSON

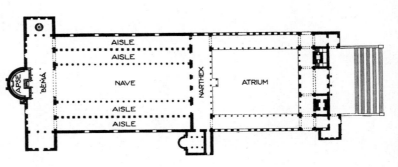

(A) *Interior of Old St. Peter's, Rome, Early 4th Century,* portion of a Renaissance fresco in S. Martino ai Monti, Rome.

P: ALINARI

(B) Plan of Old St. Peter's, Rome

Interior, St. Paul Outside the Walls, 4th Century. Rome. [Etching by G. B. Piranesi, 1749, Metropolitan Museum of Art, New York (Jacob S. Rogers Fund)]

(A) Interior, S. Maria Maggiore. 432–440 A.D. (the ceiling c. 1500). Rome. P: ANDERSON

(B) S. Apollinare
in Classe (aerial view).
c. 530–549 A.D. Ravenna.
P: FOTOCIELO, ROME

(A) Interior, S. Apollinare in Classe. Ravenna. P: ANDERSON

(B) Nave Wall, S. Apollinare Nuovo. C. 520 A.D. Ravenna. P: ANDERSON

Church at Kalb Lauzeh. c. 500 A.D. Syria. P: H. C. BUTLER,
COURTESY DEPARTMENT OF ART AND ARCHAEOLOGY, PRINCETON UNIVERSITY

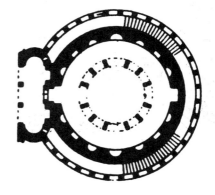

Interior and Plan, S. Costanza.
Early 4th century A.D. Rome. P: HIRMER

S. Vitale. 526–547 A.D. Ravenna. P: KIDDER SMITH (BELOW) AND EDIZIONE E. S., RAVENNA

(A) ANTHEMIUS OF TRALLES and ISIDORUS OF MILETUS. Hagia Sophia.
532–537 A.D. Istanbul (Constantinople). P: KIDDER SMITH

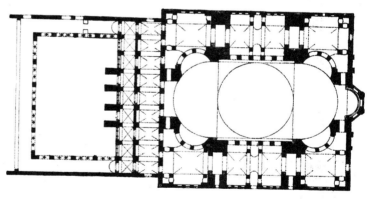

(B, C) Plan and section of
Hagia Sophia. (After V. Sybel)

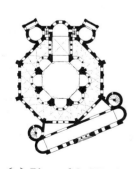

(D) Plan of S. Vitale,
Ravenna

Interior, Hagia Sophia. Istanbul. P: HIRMER

Façade and aerial view, St. Mark's. Begun 1063. Venice.
P: KIDDER SMITH (ABOVE) AND FOTOCIELO, ROME

Interior, St. Mark's. Venice. P: ANDERSON

Churches of the Monastery of Hosios Loukas (St. Luke of Stiris).
Early 11th century. Phocis, Greece. P: FRANTZ

Interior, Katholikon, Hosios Loukas. P: FRANTZ

St. Basil. 1554–60. MOSCOW. P: COURTESY THAMES & HUDSON, LTD., LONDON, FROM MARTIN HÜRLIMANN, *Moscow and Leningrad*, 1958

(B) *Portrait of Eutropios*,
from Ephesus. C. 450 A.D.
Marble, 12½″.
Kunsthistorisches Museum,
Vienna

(A) *The Good Shepherd.*
C. 350 A.D. Marble, 39″.
Lateran Museums, Rome.
P: HIRMER

(A) *Sarcophagus of Junius Bassus.* C. 359 A.D. Marble, 46½ x 95".
Vatican Grottoes, Rome. P: HIRMER

(B) *Sarcophagus of Archbishop Theodorus.* 6th century A.D. Marble, 39½ x 81".
S. Apollinare in Classe, Ravenna. P: ANDERSON

Christ Enthroned (detail of p. 237 A). P: ANDERSON

(B) *The Archangel Michael*
(leaf of a diptych).
c. 518 A.D. Ivory, 17 x 5½".
British Museum, London

(A) *The Marys at the Sepulchre*
(leaf of a diptych).
c. 400 A.D. Ivory, 12½ x 5¼".
Castello Sforzesco, Milan.

P: ARCHIVIO FOTOGRAFICO
CIVICI MUSEI, MILAN

Emperor on Horseback and Scenes of Victory (leaf of a consular diptych). c. 500–520 A.D.
Ivory, 13½ x 10½". The Louvre, Paris. P: HIRMER

OPPOSITE PAGE

Bishop's Chair (Cathedra of Maximianus). c. 520–550 A.D. Ivory on wood, 47".
Archiepiscopal Museum, Ravenna. P: HIRMER

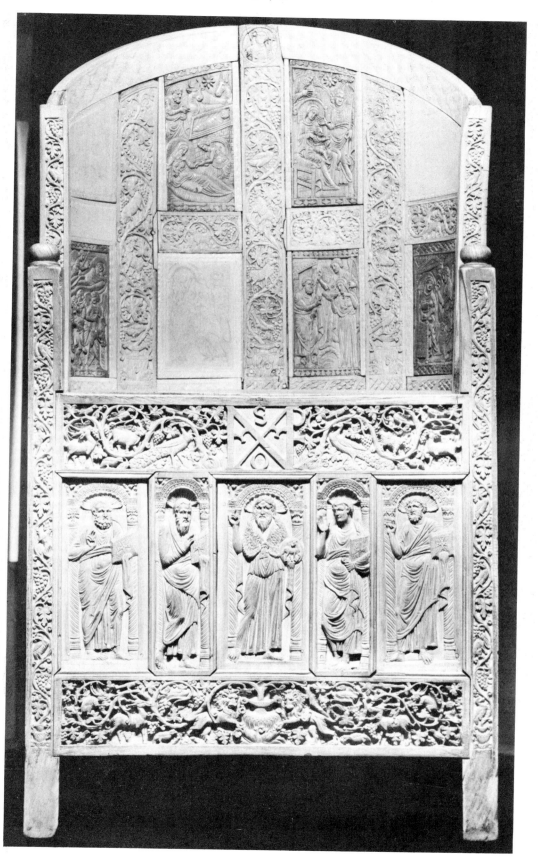

Consular Diptych of Anastasius. 517 A.D. Ivory, each leaf 14 x 5″.
Bibliothèque Nationale, Paris. P: GIRAUDON

(A) *The Harbaville Triptych.* c. 1000. Ivory, 9½ x 11". The Louvre, Paris. P: ALINARI

(B) *Adam.* 10th century.
Ivory, 2¾ x 3⅛".
Walters Art Gallery,
Baltimore

(A) *The Good Shepherd and the Story of Jonah* (painted ceiling). 3rd century A.D. Catacomb of SS. Pietro e Marcellino, Rome. P: PONTIFICIA COMMISSIONE DI ARCHEOLOGIA SACRA

(B) *Velatio* (lunette). 3rd century A.D. Catacomb of Priscilla, Rome. P: PONTIFICIA COMMISSIONE DI ARCHEOLOGIA SACRA

Madonna (detail of icon). 6th or 7th century A.D. Encaustic on wood.
S. Francesca Romana, Rome. P: GFN

Crucifixion (fresco). c. 750 A.D. S. Maria Antiqua, Rome. P: ALINARI

OPPOSITE PAGE
Madonna Enthroned. 13th century. Panel, 32 x 19½″.
National Gallery of Art, Washington, D.C. (Mellon Collection)

Miniature from the *Vatican Virgil*. c. 400 A.D. Vatican Library. Rome

Jacob Wrestling with the Angel, from the *Vienna Genesis*. Early 6th century. A.D. National Library, Vienna.

P: BILDARCHIV OESTERR. NATIONALBIBLIOTHEK

David Composing the Psalms, from the *Paris Psalter*. 10th century?
Bibliothèque Nationale, Paris

Dome Mosaic (detail). Late 4th or early 5th century A.D.
St. George, Salonika. P: HIRMER

MAXIMIANVS

Justinian and Attendants (mosaic). c. 547 A.D. S. Vitale, Ravenna. P: ANDERSON

Madonna between Constantine and Justinian (mosaic). c. 1000. Hagia Sophia, Istanbul.

P: THE BYZANTINE INSTITUTE OF AMERICA, COURTESY PAUL A. UNDERWOOD

Christ Entering Jerusalem
(mosaic). 11th century.
Daphni, Greece. p: ALINARI

Christ in Majesty
(apse mosaic). c. 1148.
Cathedral, Cefalù,
Sicily. P: BROGI

Scenes from Genesis (mosaic). c. 1200. St. Mark's, Venice. P: ALINARI

Christ in Limbo (fresco). Early 14th century. Kariye Camii, Istanbul.
P: THE BYZANTINE INSTITUTE OF AMERICA, COURTESY PAUL A. UNDERWOOD

(A) ANDREI RUBLEV.
Old Testament Trinity.
C. 1410–20. Panel,
55½ x 44½″.
Tretyakov Gallery,
Moscow

(B) *Portrait of
Ivan the Terrible.*
1547–65. Panel,
14 x 13¼″.
National Museum
of Denmark, Copenhagen

PART TWO

ASIA AND AMERICA

LIST OF ILLUSTRATIONS

12. AMERICAN ART BEFORE COLUMBUS

ASIA AND AMERICA

9. *Islamic Art*

Incense Burner (Persian), from Khurasan. 1181–82. Bronze, 33½″.
Metropolitan Museum of Art, New York (Rogers Fund, 1951)

(A) Mosque of Mutawakkil. 846–852 A.D. Samarra, Iraq. P: COURTESY CLARENDON PRESS, OXFORD, FROM K.A.C. CRESWELL, *Early Muslim Architecture*

(B) Detail, Façade of a Palace from Mshatta, Syria. 742 A.D. Formerly State Museums, Berlin

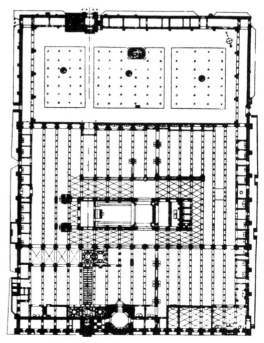

Interior and Plan, Mosque.
785–990 A.D. Cordova, Spain.
P: KIDDER SMITH

Interior, Capilla de Villaviciosa, Mosque. Cordova. P: MAS

Court of the Lions. Late 14th century (the fountain 11th century).
Alhambra Palace, Granada. P: KIDDER SMITH

Stucco Decoration, Hall of the Two Sisters. 13th century.
Alhambra Palace. P: MAS

Madrasa of Sultan Hasan. 1356–63. Cairo. P: KIDDER SMITH

Court, Madrasa of Sultan Hasan. Cairo. P: KIDDER SMITH

Mosque of Sultan Ahmed I. 1609–16. Istanbul. P: KIDDER SMITH

Taj Mahal. 1630–48. Agra, India.
P: TIERS, FROM MONKMEYER PRESS PHOTO SERVICE, NEW YORK

Landscape Mosaics. 715 A.D. The Great Mosque, Damascus, Syria.

P: COURTESY CLARENDON PRESS, OXFORD, FROM K. A. C. CRESWELL, *Early Muslim Architecture*

Coronation Cloak of the German Emperors. (Arabic workmanship, made in Palermo for Roger II of Sicily). 1133–34. Red silk and gold embroidery, 11′2″. Weltliche Schatzkammer, Kunsthistorisches Museum, Vienna

ABOVE

OPPOSITE PAGE, ABOVE

(A) *Banner Bearers and Trumpeters*, from a Hariri Manuscript from Baghdad 1237. Bibliothèque Nationale, Paris

OPPOSITE PAGE, BELOW

(B) *A Dispute*, from a Hariri Manuscript. Mesopotamian, c. 1250. British Museum, London

واشرت الى الدرهم فوى بالسر المضهر وان البين ان نرى خذى الفطعة واسيرجن

Two Warriors Fighting in a Landscape, from a Persian Manuscript, 1396.
British Museum, London

ASIA AND AMERICA·

10. *Art of Indian Asia*

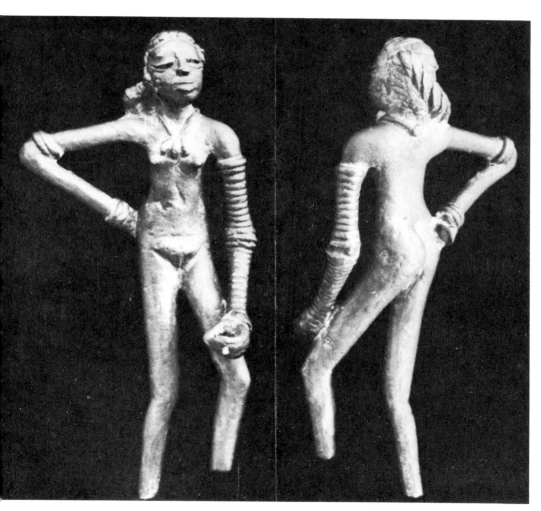

Statuette of a Dancer, from Mohenjo-Daro. c. 3000–1500 B.C. Copper, 4¼".
Archeological Museum, Mohenjo-Daro. P: DEPT. ARCH. INDIA

(A) *Three Seals,*
from Mohenjo-Daro.
C. 3000–1500 B.C.
Archeological Museum,
Mohenjo-Daro.
P: DEPT. ARCH. INDIA

(B) *Lion Capital,* from a column erected by King Aśoka.
242–232 B.C. Stone, 7′. Museum, Sarnath.
P: DEPT. ARCH. INDIA

Stūpa No. 1. 3rd–1st century B.C. Sānchī. P: ELISOFON

North Gate, Stūpa No. 1. Early 1st century B.C. Sānchī. P: ELISOFON

The Parinirvāna of the Buddha (detail of p. 282). P: ELISOFON

Yakshī, from East Gate Stūpa No. 1. Early 1st century B.C. Sānchī. P: ELISOFON

Seated Buddha, from Gandhāra. 3rd century A.D. Schist, 36″. Seattle Art Museum

The Fasting Buddha, from Gandhāra. 2nd or 3rd century A.D.
Central Museum, Lahore, Pakistan

(B) *The Buddha Subdues the Mad Elephant* (railing medallion from a stūpa), from Amarāvatī. 2nd century A.D. Marble, 3 1/2". Government Museum, Madras. P: GOLOUBEV, GUIMET

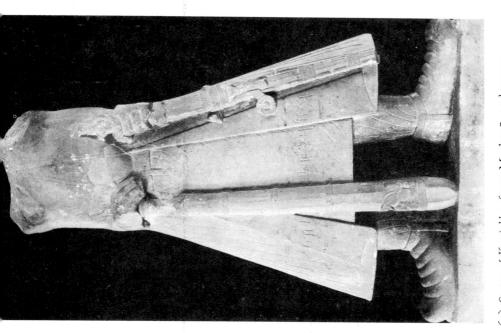

(A) *Statue of Kanishka*, from Mathurā. 2nd century A.D. Museum of Archeology, Mathurā. P: DEPT. ARCH. INDIA

Standing Buddha,
from Mathurā.
5th century.
85½″. Indian Museu
Calcutta.
P: LARKIN BROS.,
LONDON

Vishnu on the Serpent Ananta. 578 A.D. Cave III,
Bādāmī. P: DEPT. ARCH. INDIA

(A) Façade, Cave No. 19. Early 6th century A.D. Ajantā. P: ELISOFON

(B) Temple No. 17. Earl
5th century A.D. Sānchī
P: DEPT. ARCH. INDIA

The Beautiful Bodhisattva (detail of wall painting). c. 600–642 A.D.
Cave No. 1, Ajantā. P: ELISOFON

Śiva as King of Dancers. Late 7th century A.D.
Cave No. 21, Elūrā. P: ELISOFON

Śiva Trinity. 8th century A.D. Śiva Cave Temple,
Elephanta. P: ELISOFON

The Great Temple Compound. 8th–13th century. Bhuvaneśvara. P: ELISOFON

Śiva as King of Dancers, from south India. 12th or 13th century. Bronze, 60½″.
Museum of Asiatic Art, Amsterdam. P: ELISOFON

(A) *Ānanda Attending the Parinirvāna of the Buddha.* 12th century. Granite, c. 23′. Gal Vihāra, Polonnāruva, Ceylon. P: MARTIN HÜRLIMANN, COURTESY BOLLINGEN FOUNDATION, INC., N.Y.

(B) Aerial View of the Stūpa. Late 8th–9th century A.D. Borobudur, Ja[...]

P: COURTESY FOGG ART MUSEUM, HARVARD UNIVERS[...]

The Flight of Manoharā, from the Story of Prince Sudhana and *The Monkey King Sugrīva*, from the Rāmayāna frieze. Stūpa, Borobudur. P: GOLOUBEV, GUIMET

(A) Aerial view of Angkor Vat. Early 12th century. Cambodia. P: ELISOFON

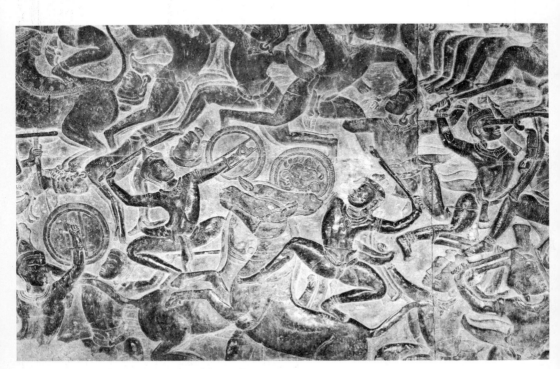

(B) *Battle of Gods and Demons.* Angkor Vat. P: ELISOFON

Female Figure, from Cambodia.
6th–7th century A.D. 57″.
Guimet Museum, Paris.
P: ELISOFON

Mucalinda Buddha. 12th century. 35½″.
Albert Sarraut Museum, Pnompenh, Cambodia. P: ELISOFON

ASIA AND AMERICA

11. Chinese and Japanese Art

Hunting and Threshing Scene, rubbing from a tomb tile from Ch'êng-tu,
Szechwan. Later Han Dynasty, 25–221 A.D. 16½ x 18″.
P: COURTESY RICHARD RUDOLPH, UNIVERSITY OF CALIFORNIA

(A) *Pottery House Model.*
Han Dynasty,
206 B.C.–221 A.D.
52″. Nelson Gallery
of Art and Atkins
Museum, Kansas City

(B) The Sanctuary,
Ise Inner Shrine.
Traditional since
the 3rd century A.D.
and periodically rebuilt.
Japan. P: (C. 1900)
BENRIDO CO., KYOTO

Pagoda. 951 A.D. Daigoji, Japan. P: ASUKAEN, NARA

Courtyard (from the southeast), Hōryūji Monastery. 7th century A.D. Japan. P: ASUKAEN, NARA

The Middle Gate (detail of p. 304). P: ASUKAEN, NARA

(B) Interior, Kondō, Tōshōdai-ji. Late 8th century A.D.
Nara. P: ASUKAEN, NARA

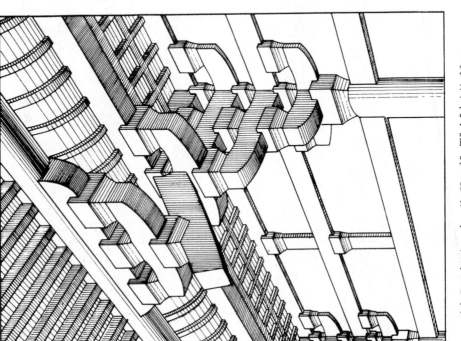

(A) Bracketing detail, Kondō, Tōshōdai-ji, Nara,
Japan. P: A. C. SOPER, The Evolution of Buddhist
Architecture in Japan. PRINCETON, 1942

Hōōdō ("Phoenix Hall"). 11th century.
Byōdō-in, Uji, Japan. P: ASUKAEN, NARA

Construction Methods, from the narrative scroll *Matsuzaki-tenjin-engi.*
1311. National Museum, Tokyo

(A) *A Priest's House,*
from the scroll *Kasuga-gongen-reikenki.*
1309. National Museum, Tokyo.
P: COURTESY A. C. SOPER, NEW YORK UNIVERSITY

(B) *House of a Gentleman,* from the scroll *Ishiyamadera-engi.* 14th century.
National Museum, Tokyo. P: COURTESY A. C. SOPER, NEW YORK UNIVERSITY

Li Jung-Chin. *A Pleasure Palace* (painting on silk). Yüan Dynasty, 1260–1368. National Palace Museum, Peking. P: COURTESY A. C. SOPER, NEW YORK UNIVERSITY

Himeji Castle. Late 16th century. Japan. P: COURTESY CITY HALL, HIMEJI

The Grand Ancestral Shrine (*T'ai-miao*) in the Peking Palace.
15th century, with later refurbishings. P: COURTESY A. C. SOPER, NEW YORK UNIVERSITY

Katsura Imperial Villa. 17th century. Japan.

P : T. SATO, TOKYO, COURTESY A. C. SOPER, NEW YORK UNIVERSITY

Interior, Kuro-shoin of the Nishi Hongan-ji. Late 16th century.
Kyoto. P: BENRIDO CO., KYOTO

Bronze Vessel (type IH). Early Chou Dynasty, c. 1000 B.C.
Freer Gallery of Art, Washington, D.C.

(A) *Dragon.* Late Chou
Dynasty, 6th–3rd century B.C.
Bronze, c. 25½″ .
Collection Jacques Stoclet,
Brussels. P: PAUL BESSEM,
AMSTERDAM

(B) *Jade Disk* (type PI).
Late Chou Dynasty,
6th–3rd century B.C. 85/8″.
Nelson Gallery
of Art and Atkins Museum,
Kansas City

Funerary Pillar of Shên.
2nd century A.D.
c. 8′9″.
Ch'ü-hsien, Szechwan.
P: GUIMET

Winged Lion, from the
Tomb of Hsiao Hsiu.
518 A.D. C. 12′.
Nanking. P: GUIMET

Camel. T'ang Dynasty, 618–906 A.D.
Clay, 10 x 11″. Rietberg Museum, Zurich
(Collection E. v. d. Heydt)

Prabhūtaratna and Sākyamuni (Buddhist Shrine). 518 A.D. Gilt bronze, 10¼″.
Guimet Museum, Paris. P: ARCH. PHOT.

Colossal Buddha, C. 450–500 A.D. C. 45′. Cave No. 20, Yün-kang, Shansi.
P: COURTESY LAURENCE SICKMAN, KANSAS CITY

Buddhist Stele. 554 A.D. 7'.
Museum of Fine Arts, Boston

(A) Detail of p. 322

(B) *Empress and Court*, from Pin-yang Cave, Lung-mên. Early 6th century. 76 x 109 ″.
Nelson Gallery of Art and Atkins Museum, Kansas City

Bodhisattva.
T'ang Dynasty,
8th century A.D. 38″.
Freer Gallery of Art,
Washington, D. C.

Lohan. Sung Dynasty, 12th century. Three-color glazed terracotta, c. 40″.
University Museum, Philadelphia

Figurine,
from Satohara
(Gumma Prefecture).
Late Jōmon,
4th–3rd century B.C.
Clay, 11¾″.
Collection Y. Yamasaki.
P: ASUKAEN, NARA

RIGHT
Warrior in Armor.
Haniwa, 6th century A.D.
Clay, 25″. Collection
Yoshio Negishi,
Saitama-ken

Miroku (Matreya)
Meditating. C. 650 A.D.
Wood, 52″.
Chūgūji Nunnery,
Nara-ken.

P: ASUKAEN, NARA

Detail of p. 332 A.

P: ASUKAEN, NARA

(A) *Eleven-Headed Kwannon*. 8th century A.D.
Dry lacquer, 82". Shōrinji,
Nara-ken. P: ASUKAEN, NARA

(B) *Jikokuten (Guardian Deity).*
8th century A.D. Clay, 64". Kaidan-in,
Todai-ji, Nara. P: ASUKAEN, NARA

Portrait of Ganjin. 763–784 A.D. Dry lacquer, 32″.
Kaisan-dō, Tōshōdai-ji, Nara. P: NATIONAL MUSEUM, TOKYO

Amida Buddha. 1252. Bronze, c. 37′4″. Kamakura.

OPPOSITE PAGE

UNKEI and FOLLOWERS. *Mūchaku.* Early 13th century. Wood, 75″.
Hokuen-dō, Kōfuku-ji, Nara

Portrait of Uesugi Shigefusa.
13th century. Wood, 27½".
Meigetsu-in, Kanagawa
Prefecture.

P: COURTESY EXHIBITION
DELEGATION, "ART TREASURES
FROM JAPAN," 1958

ABOVE

(C) *Kyogen Mask (O Oji)*.
15th century. Wood, 7⅛".
National Museum, Tokyo

LEFT

(B) *Nō Mask (Horai Onna)*.
16th century. Wood, 8⅜".
National Museum, Tokyo

LEFT

(A) *Bugaku Mask (Ryō-ō)*.
13th century. Wood, 15".
Kanzeon-ji, Fukuoka.
P: COURTESY EXHIBITION DELEGATION,
"ART TREASURES FROM JAPAN," 1958

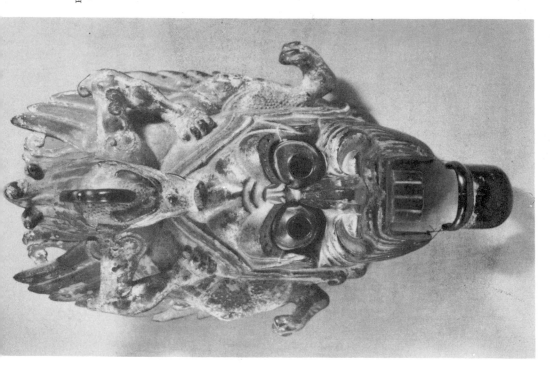

Procession of Dignitaries, wall painting from a tomb. Later Han Dynasty, 2nd century A.D. Liao-yang, Manchuria. P: COURTESY LAURENCE SICKMAN, KANSAS CITY

OPPOSITE PAGE

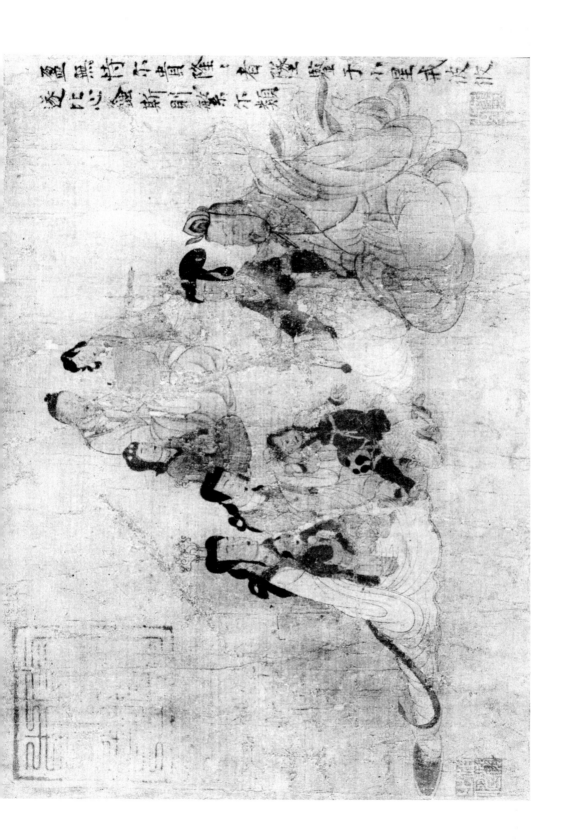

Landscape (detail of wall painting). Early 8th century A.D. Cave No. 70,
Tun-huang. P: COURTESY LAURENCE SICKMAN, KANSAS CITY

Palace Ladies Tuning the Lute and Drinking Tea. 10th or 11th century version of a design attributed to Chou Fang (c. 800 A.D.). Scroll painting on silk, 11 x 29½″. Nelson Gallery of Art and Atkins Museum, Kansas City

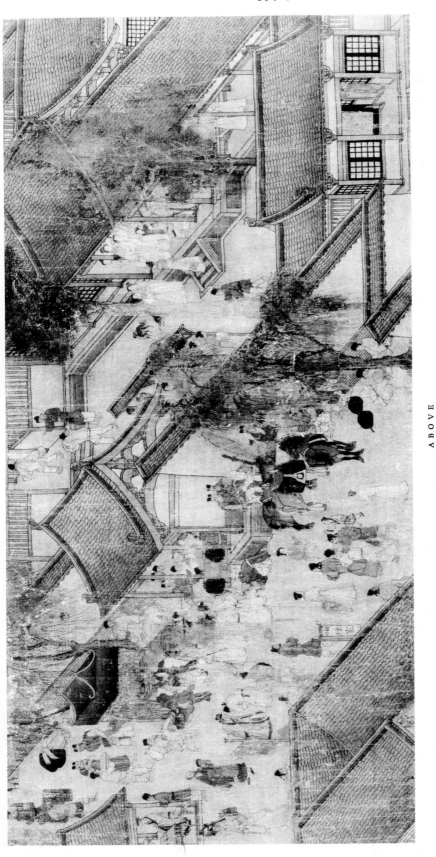

ABOVE

The Return of Lady Wên-chi from Captivity in Mongolia. 12th century. Painting on silk,
10 x 22". Museum of Fine Arts, Boston

OPPOSITE PAGE

Hsü Tao-ning. *Fishing in a Mountain Stream* (detail). 11th century. Ink drawing on silk, 19 x 82".
Nelson Gallery of Art and Atkins Museum, Kansas City

MA YÜAN. *Bare Willows and Distant Mountains.* c. 1190–1224. Painting on paper, 9½".
Museum of Fine Arts, Boston

LIANG K'AI (or EARLY JAPANESE COPY?) *The Sixth Patriarch, Hui-néng, Tearing up the Sutras.*
13th century. Ink drawing on paper, 28 x 12½". National Museum, Tokyo

Dragon Vase (Tz'u chou ware). Sung Dynasty, 10th–13th century. 22½″.
Nelson Gallery of Art and Atkins Museum, Kansas City

CH'ÊN JUNG. *Nine Dragon Scroll* (details). 1244. Ink and slight color on paper, 18¼" x 35'10". Museum of Fine Arts, Boston

ABOVE

LI K'AN. *Bamboo* (detail). Late 13th century. Ink on paper, 14¾ x 93½".
Nelson Gallery of Art and Atkins Museum, Kansas City

OPPOSITE PAGE

Muijū-rikiku. 9th–10th century A.D. Painting on silk, 10'8½" x 5'11". Yūshi Hachimankō,
Wakayama. P: COURTESY EXHIBITION DELEGATION, "ART TREASURES FROM JAPAN," 1958

Animal Scrolls (details). 12th century. Ink on paper, 12″. Kōzan-ji, Kyoto.

Scroll of the Hungry Ghosts (*Gaki Zōshi*) (details). c. 1200. Painting on paper, 11¼″ x 17′8″.
National Commission for Protection of Cultural Properties, Japan.

FUJIWARA TAKANOBU. *Portrait of Yoritomo.* Late 12th century. Painting on silk, 54 x 44″.
Jingoji, Kyoto. P: ASUKAEN, NARA

Portrait of Gonzō (detail). 12th century copy of a 9th century original.
Painting on silk, 66 x 54″. Fumon-in, Kōyasan, Wakayama Prefecture.
P: COURTESY EXHIBITION DELEGATION, "ART TREASURES FROM JAPAN," 1958

The Burning of the Sanjō Palace (detail). 13th century. Scroll painting on paper, 16" x 23'. Museum of Fine Arts, Boston

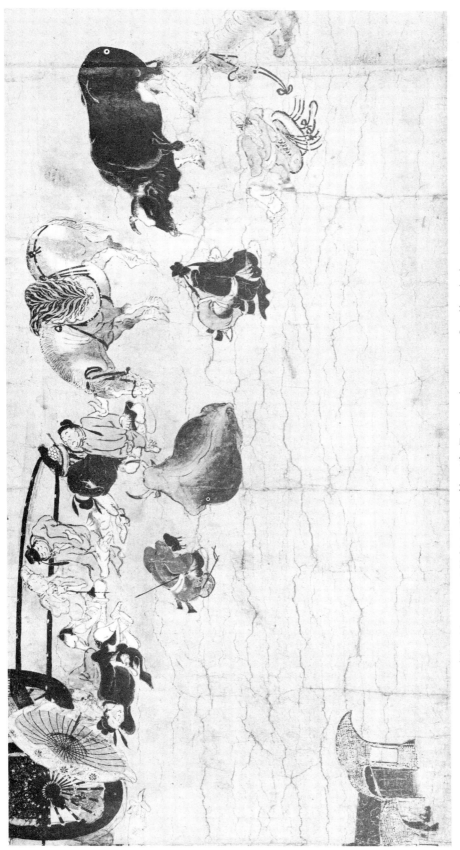

The Adventures of Kibi in China (detail). Early 13th century. Scroll painting on paper, 12″ x 80′. Museum of Fine Arts, Boston

三會龍華未厭當
長街短巷恣徉徉
布袋裏許乾坤大
拄丈頭邊日月長
兜率陀天乾屋振
毗盧樓閣水雲鄉
寄言我是真彌勒
寥廓無端向外揚

玉几　正印禪黃

MOKUAN. *Hotei*. Early
14th century. Ink on
paper, 45″. Collection K.
Sumimoto, Japan.

P: COURTESY R. T. PAINE,
MUSEUM OF FINE ARTS, BOSTON

SESSHŪ. *Winter Landscape*. Late 15th century. Ink on paper,
18 x 11½". National Museum, Tokyo

HAGESAWA TŌHAKU. *Pines* (detail), from a screen. Late 16th century.
Ink on paper, 61″. National Museum, Tokyo.

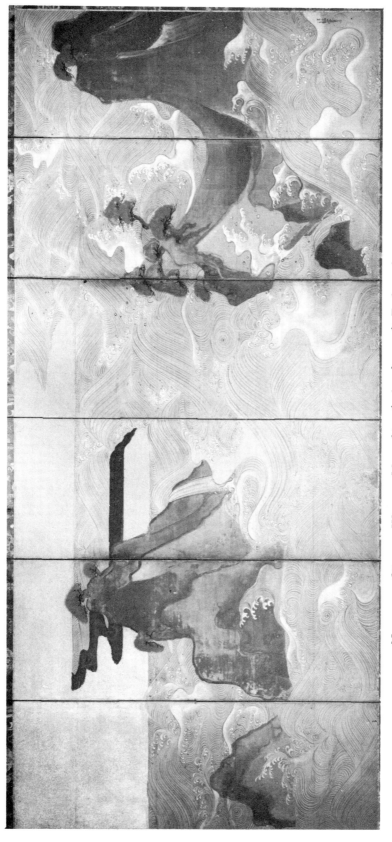

NONOMURA SŌSATSU. *Waves at Matsushima* (painted screen). Early 17th century.
Paper, 65½" . Freer Gallery of Art, Washington, D. C.

LEFT
(A) *Bishamonten* (woodcut). 1162.
Museum of Fine Arts, Boston

BELOW
(B) KAIGETSUDŌ ANCHI.
A Famous Beauty
(woodcut). c. 1710.
The Art Institute of Chicago

Kitagawa Utamaro.
*House Cleaning at the End
of the Year* (two of five scenes).
c. 1800. Nelson Gallery of Art
and Atkins Museum,
Kansas City

(A) TOSHUSAI SHARAKU.
The Actor Otani Oniji III
(in a role of October 14, 1794).
The Art Institute of Chicago

(B) ANDŌ HIROSHIGE.
Light Showers at Shono (woodcut)
1833.
Nelson Gallery of Art
and Atkins Museum, Kansas City

ASIA AND AMERICA

12. American Art before Columbus

Gesturing Figure, from Colima, Mexico. c. 500–900 A.D.
Clay, 11″. Museum of Primitive Art, New York

Mayan Palace and Temple. 11th–12th century. Labná, Yucatan.

P: COURTESY LORING HEWEN, NEW YORK

Detail of p. 366 A.

P: CARNEGIE INSTITUTION OF WASHINGTON, WASHINGTON, D.C.

(A) Temple of the Warriors. 11th century. Chichen Itzá, Yucatan.
P: © LAURA GILPIN, SANTA FE, NEW MEXICO

(B) *Chacmool*, from Chichen Itzá. 42″. National Museum,
Mexico City. P: INA MEXICO

Temple of Quetzalcoatl. 9th century A.D. Teotihuacán,
Mexico. P: INA MEXICO

Inca Citadel. 15th century. Machu Picchu, Peru.
P: COURTESY PÁL KELEMEN, from *Medieval American Art*

(A) Masonry. 15th century. Ollantaytambo, Peru. P: H. UBBELOHDE-DOERING

(B) "Gateway of the Sun." c. 1000–1300. Tihuanaco, Bolivia.
P: COURTESY PÁL KELEMEN, FROM *Medieval American Art*

The Corn God,
detail of
Stele No. 40, from
Piedras Negras.
Mayan,
8th century A.D.
National Museum,
Guatemala City.
P: UNIVERSITY
MUSEUM,
PHILADELPHIA

(A) *Arraignment of Prisoners* (watercolor copy), Mayan wall painting.
6th century A.D. Bonampak, Mexico. P: INA MEXICO

(B) Detail of A (photograph showing condition at the time of discovery).
P: GILES G. HEALY, COURTESY PÁL KELEMEN, FROM *Medieval American Art*

ABOVE

Wrestler (Olmec), from Uxpanapan. 1st century B.C.? 26″.
Private collection, Mexico City. P: GROTH-KIMBALL

OPPOSITE PAGE

Coatlicue (*Goddess of Earth and Death*). Aztec, 15th century. 99″.
National Museum, Mexico City. P: GROTH-KIMBALL

Seated Female Figure (Quimbaya), from Cauca, Colombia. c. 1000–1300. Gold, 11½″.
Museo Arqueológico y de America, Madrid. P: COURTESY CONNAISSANCE DES ARTS, PARIS

Battle of Bean Warriors (stirrup-spout jar). Mochica,
c. 400–1000. The Art Institute of Chicago

LEFT

(A) Beaker (Chimu).
c. 1300–1438. Gold, 6½″.
The Art Institute of Chicago

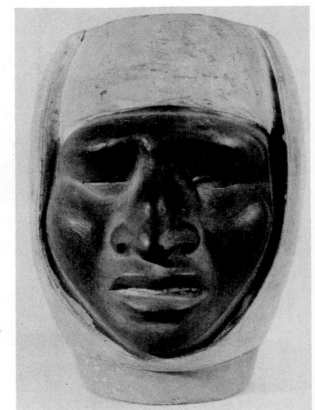

RIGHT

(B) Portrait Jar (Mochica).
c. 400–1000. Clay, 4⅛″.
Collection Norbert Mayrock,
Santiago, Chile

PART THREE

THE MIDDLE AGES

LIST OF ILLUSTRATIONS

13. EARLY MEDIEVAL ART

14. ROMANESQUE ART

15. GOTHIC ART NORTH OF THE ALPS

THE MIDDLE AGES

13. Early Medieval Art

Balustrade Relief Inscribed with the Name of the Patriarch Sigvald (now part of Baptismal Font). 762–776 A.D. C. 3 x 5′. Cathedral, Cividale, Italy. P: BRISIGHELLI, UDINE

LEFT

(A) Church Tower. c. 1000.
Earl's Barton, Northamptonshire,
England. P: KERSTING

BELOW

(B) Monastery Gate. Begun 767 A.D.
Lorsch, Germany.
P: SCHMIDT-GLASSNER

Interior and plan of the Chapel
of Charlemagne. Consecrated 805 A.D.
Aachen (Aix-la-Chapelle). P: SBB

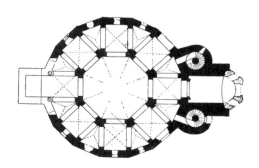

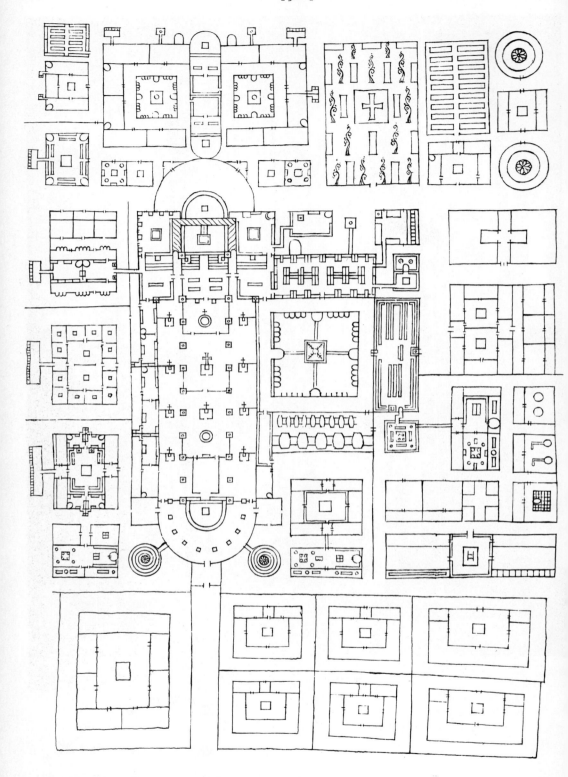

Ideal Plan of the Monastery of St. Gall. Before 830 A.D. Stiftsbibliothek, St. Gall, Switzerland.
P: COURTESY WALTER HORN, BERKELEY, CAL.

West Façade ("Westwerk"), Monastery Church. 873–885 A.D. Corvey, Germany.

View and plan of St. Michael's.
1001–33. Hildesheim,
Germany. P: SBB

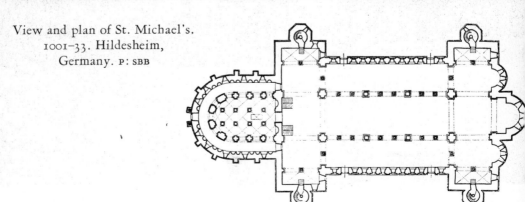

(A) Gold and Enamel Purse Cover, from the Sutton Hoo Ship-Burial, Suffolk.
Before 655 A.D. British Museum, London

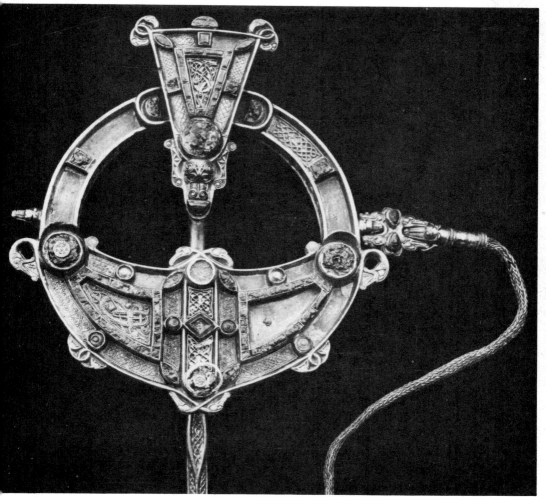

(B) *The Tara Brooch* (portion). Early 8th century A.D. National Museum, Dublin.

P: IRISH TATLER & SKETCH, DUBLIN

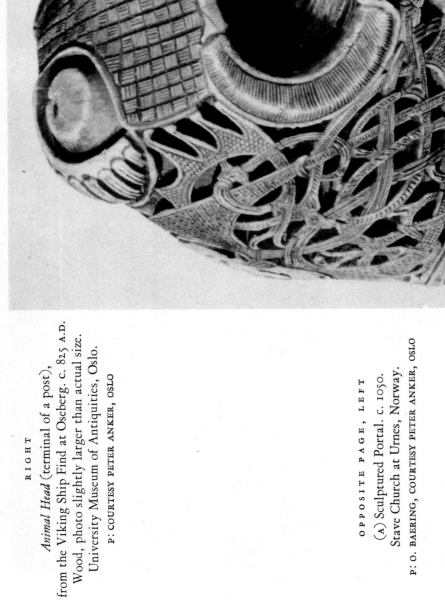

RIGHT

Animal Head (terminal of a post),
from the Viking Ship Find at Oseberg. c. 825 A.D.
Wood, photo slightly larger than actual size.
University Museum of Antiquities, Oslo.

P: COURTESY PETER ANKER, OSLO

OPPOSITE PAGE, LEFT
(A) Sculptured Portal. c. 1050.
Stave Church at Urnes, Norway.
P: O. BAERING, COURTESY PETER ANKER, OSLO

OPPOSITE PAGE, RIGHT
(B) Ornamented Page, from
the *Book of Durrow*.
Late 7th century A.D.
Trinity College Library, Dublin

Charlemagne? 9th century A.D. Bronze statuette.
The Louvre, Paris. P: GIRAUDON

Front Cover of the *Lindau Gospels*. c. 870 A.D. Gold and jewels.
The Pierpont Morgan Library, New York

Adam and Eve Reproached by the Lord and *Cain Slaying Abel*,
details of the bronze doors of Bishop Bernward. 1015. Each c. 23 x 43″.
Hildesheim Cathedral, Germany. P: WEHMEYER, HILDESHEIM

Crucifix. Late 11th century. Bronze, 43″. Parish Church,
Werden-Essen, Germany. P: ANN BREDOL-LEPPER, AACHEN

The Gero Crucifix. c. 975–1000. Wood, 74″.
Cathedral, Cologne. P: MARBURG

ABOVE

(A) *Christ and the Doubting Thomas.* C. 990 A.D. Ivory, 9½ x 4″. Formerly State Museums, Berlin

RIGHT

(B) *Tomb Slab of Rudolf of Swabia.* C. 1080–1100. Bronze, 77½ x 27″. Cathedral, Merseburg, Germany.

P: SBB

Cross Page, from the *Lindisfarne Gospels*. C. 700 A.D.
British Museum, London

Initial Page (*XPI*), from the *Book of Kells*. Late 8th century A.D.
Trinity College Library, Dublin. P: LENSMEN PRESS, DUBLIN

Symbol of St. Mark, from the *Echternach Gospels*.
Early 8th century A.D. Bibliothèque Nationale, Paris

The Crucifixion, from an Irish Gospel Book. c. 750–760 A.D.
Stiftsbibliothek, St. Gall, Switzerland

(B) *St. Mark*, from the *Gospel Book of Ebbo of Reims*. 816-835 A.D. Municipal Library, Épernay, France

(A) *St. Matthew*, from the *Gospel Book of Charlemagne*. c. 800 A.D. Schatzkammer, Kunsthistorisches Museum, Vienna

[405]

Illustration to Psalm 44, from the *Utrecht Psalter*. c. 832 A.D. University Library, Utrecht

The Annunciation, from a Sacramentary formerly at St. Gereon, Cologne. c. 990–1000.
Bibliothèque Nationale, Paris. P: MARBURG

The Angel with the Millstone, from the *Bamberg Apocalypse*. C. 1020.
Bavarian State Library, Munich. P: HIRMER

Initial Page of the Gospel of St. Luke, from a French Gospel Book.
c. 1000. The Pierpont Morgan Library, New York

THE MIDDLE AGES

14. Romanesque Art

The Abbey Church of Cluny Before 1798, detail of a watercolor by J.-B. Lallemand.
Bibliothèque Nationale, Paris

Crossing Tower and Choir. Begun early 11th century.
St. Philibert, Tournus, France. P: ARCH. PHOT.

Interior, St. Philibert. Tournus. P: ROUBIER

Abbey Church. 1040–67. Jumièges, France. P: MARBURG

West Façade. Begun c. 1050. St. Etienne, Caen, France. P: ROUBIER

Nave and Choir, St. Etienne. Caen. P: ROUBIER

Nave. 1093-1130. Durham Cathedral, England. P: KERSTING

West Façade. Early 12th century. Notre-Dame-La-Grande, Poitiers, France.

P: MARTIN HÜRLIMANN, FROM *France*, LONDON, THAMES & HUDSON, 1957

Nave. Begun c. 1080. St. Savin-sur-Gartempe, France. P: ROUBIER

Tournai Cathedral. Nave completed 1171. Belgium. P: ACL

(B) Aerial view of St. Sernin, Toulouse, France.
P: YAN, TOULOUSE

(A) Aerial view of St. Front, Périgueux, France.
P: COMPAGNIE AÉRIENNE FRANÇAISE, SURESNES

Interior, St. Front. c. 1125–50. Périgueux. P: ROUBIER

Nave. Early 12th century. St. Sernin, Toulouse. P: ROUBIER

Nave Wall. Early 12th century. St. Lazare, Autun, France. P: ROUBIER

Speyer Cathedral. Begun 1030. Germany. P: SBB

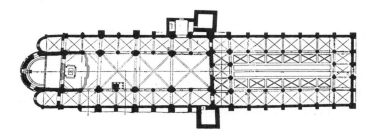

View and plan of S. Ambrogio.
c. 1125–50. Milan. P: ALINARI

Interior,
S. Ambrogio.
Milan. P: ALINARI

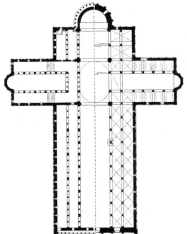

View and plan of Pisa Cathedral.
Begun 1063. Italy.
P: KIDDER SMITH

Nave, Pisa Cathedral. P: ALINARI

ABOVE

Baptistery. Begun c. 1060. Florence. P: ALINARI

OPPOSITE PAGE

Christ in Glory. c. 1090. St. Sernin, Toulouse. P: ROUBIER

South Portal (portion). Early 12th century. St. Pierre,
Moissac, France. P: ARCH. PHOT.

South Portal (detail). Early 12th century.
St. Pierre, Moissac. P: MARBURG

ABOVE

Last Judgment (detail of west tympanum). Early 12th century.
St. Lazare, Autun. P: BULLOZ

OPPOSITE PAGE, ABOVE

(A) *Lion Monument.* Erected by Duke Henry the Lion, 1166.
Bronze, c. 73″ long. Cathedral Square, Brunswick, Germany.
P: COURTESY THE WARBURG INSTITUTE, UNIVERSITY OF LONDON

OPPOSITE PAGE, BELOW

(B) REGNIER OF HUY. *The Baptism of Christ* (baptismal font). c. 1110. Bronze, 25″.
St. Barthélemy, Liège, Belgium. P: ACL

The Mission to the Apostles, tympanum of the central portal of the Narthex.
1120–32.
Ste. Madeleine,
Vézelay, France.

P: BULLOZ

MASTER WILIGELMUS and ASSISTANTS. *Scenes from Genesis.* C. 1110.
Façade, Cathedral, Modena, Italy. P: ALINARI

Detail of p. 437 A. P: MARBURG

(A) West Portals. Early 12th century. Abbey Church,
St. Gilles du Gard, France. P: ROUBIER

(B) MASTER ROBERTUS. *Events from the Life of Moses* (portion of baptismal font).
c. 1190. Marble, c. 30″. S. Frediano, Lucca, Italy. P: H. W. JANSON

Episcopal Throne. Early 12th century (or 1098?).
Marble. S. Nicola, Bari, Italy.
P: HANS DECKER, FROM *Romanesque Art in Italy*

Jonah and the Whale (marble relief). c. 1260. Cathedral,
Sessa Aurunca, Italy. P: GFN

BENEDETTO ANTELAMI. *King David*. c. 1180–90. Cathedral Façade, Borgo San Donnino,
Italy. P: COURTESY GEZA DE FRANCOVICH, ROME

The Adoration of the Magi
(Anglo-Norman). c. 1140. Whalebone,
height 14½″, greatest width 6¼″.
Victoria and Albert Museum,
London

Embarkation of William, Battle of Hastings, and *Death of Harold,* details from
the *Bayeux Tapestry.* c. 1073–83. Wool embroidery on linen, 20″ wide
(the whole, 230′ long). Town Hall, Bayeux, France. P: GIRAUDON

St. Matthew, from a Gospel Book produced at Corbie. c. 1025–50.
Municipal Library, Amiens. P: ARCH. PHOT.

The Building of the Tower of Babel, detail of the vault of the nave. Early 12th century. Fresco. St.-Savin-sur-Gartempe (see p. 417). P: PIERRE DEVINOY, PARIS

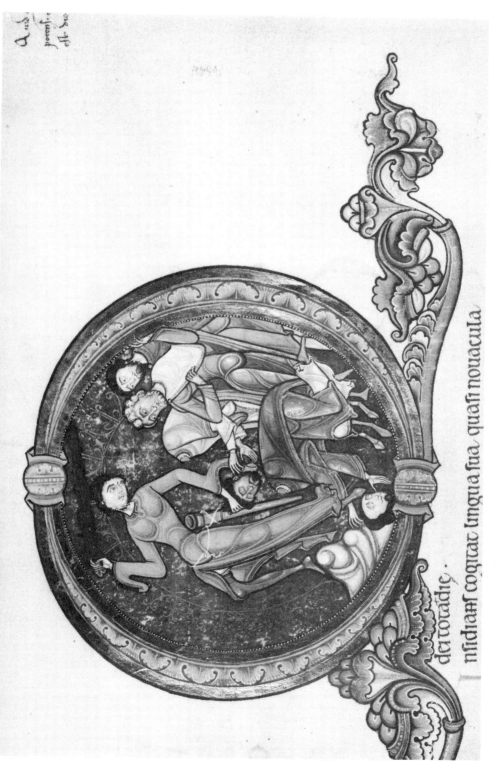

Doëg Slaying the Priests, figured initial from the *Winchester Bible*.
c. 1150–60. Cathedral Library, Winchester

The Harmony of the Spheres, from a manuscript of c. 1170.
Municipal Library, Reims. P: ARCH. PHOT.

Que reƈ ſƈ obliuiſcens ao deſtinatū ꝛcɛdo bīuū
ſupꝛne uocatioīs. ƈƈ d̅n̅s in euanglio dic̅. Dimitte
mortuoſ ſepelire mortuoſ. tu au̅ uade. ſeꝗꝛe me.

Tigris uocata ꝓpƈ uoluc̅ƈ fugā. ita H no
minant pſe. gꝛeci. œ medi ſagittā. ſit en̅
beſtia uariis diſtincta maclis. ūtute œ uelo
citate mirabit̅. ex cuꝯ noīe flum̅ tigs̅ appellat.
q̅o̅ his rapidiſſim̅ ſit om̅m̅ū fluuioꝛ. has mag̅
hircania gignit. Tygs̅ u̅ u̅ uacuū rapte ſobo

Tiger Licking Her Image in a Mirror while a Hunter Steals Her Cub,
from an English bestiary manuscript. c. 1185.
The Pierpont Morgan Library, New York

David and Daniel (stained glass windows). c. 1100–20. 90½″.
Cathedral, Augsburg, Germany. P: COURTESY HANS WENTZEL, STUTTGART

The Virgin with Apostles, detail of *The Ascension* (stained glass window). c. 1150. 74 x 45".
Le Mans Cathedral, France. P: ARCH. PHOT.

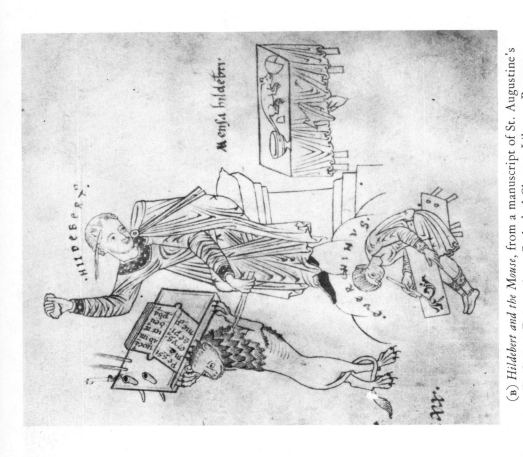

(B) *Hildebert and the Mouse*, from a manuscript of St. Augustine's
De Civitate Dei. 1136–37. Cathedral Chapter Library, Prague.
P: STATE ADM. OF MON., FORMERLY PHOTOMETRIC INST., PRAGUE

(A) *Spring Landscape*, from a manuscript of *Carmina Burana.*
Early 13th century. Bavarian State Library, Munich

THE MIDDLE AGES

15. Gothic Art
North of the Alps

The Kiss of Judas, from the Choir Screen. c. 1250-60.
Naumburg Cathedral, Germany. P: MARBURG

(B) Interior, Ambulatory. 1140–44. Abbey Church of
St. Denis. P: PIERRE DEVINOY, PARIS

(A) Abbey Church of St. Denis. Paris. Consecrated 1144.
(After an early 19th-century print showing façade prior to 1833).

West Portals. c. 1145–70. Chartres Cathedral, France. P: MARBURG

West Façade and Plan of Notre Dame. 1163–c. 1250. Paris. P: WARD

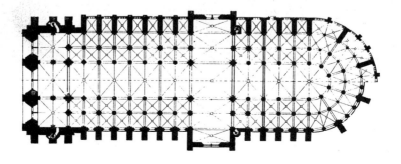

Nave. 1163–c. 1200. Notre Dame, Paris. P: ROUBIER

Nave. 1194–1220. Chartres Cathedral. P: MARBURG

Choir Vault. Completed 1247. Amiens Cathedral, France. P: WARD

Notre Dame (view from the southeast).
Paris. P: KIDDER SMITH

Façade. 1225–36. Amiens Cathedral.
(Towers 14th and 15th century).

P: KIDDER SMITH

West Façade. Mid-13th–15th century. Reims Cathedral,
France. P: MARBURG

Interior. Begun 1247. Beauvais Cathedral, France.

P: WARD

LEFT

(A) Aerial view of
Beauvais Cathedral.

P. INSTITUT
GÉOGRAPHIQUE
NATIONAL,
CENTRE DE
DOCUMENTATION
DE PHOTOGRAPHIES
AÉRIENNES, PARIS

BELOW

(B) St. Urbain. 1261–75.
Troyes, France.

P: MARTIN HÜRLIMANN,
FROM *France*, LONDON,
THAMES & HUDSON, 1957

West Façade. 13th–16th century. Rouen Cathedral,
France. P: WARD

View and plan of Salisbury Cathedral. 1220–70.
England. P: EDWIN SMITH

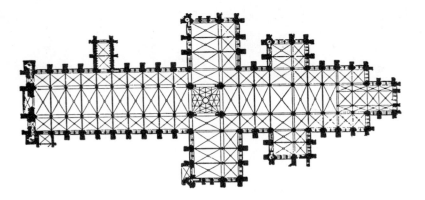

Nave, Salisbury Cathedral. P: F. H. CROSSLEY, NBR LONDON

Arches of the crossing. 1338. Wells Cathedral,
England. P: KERSTING

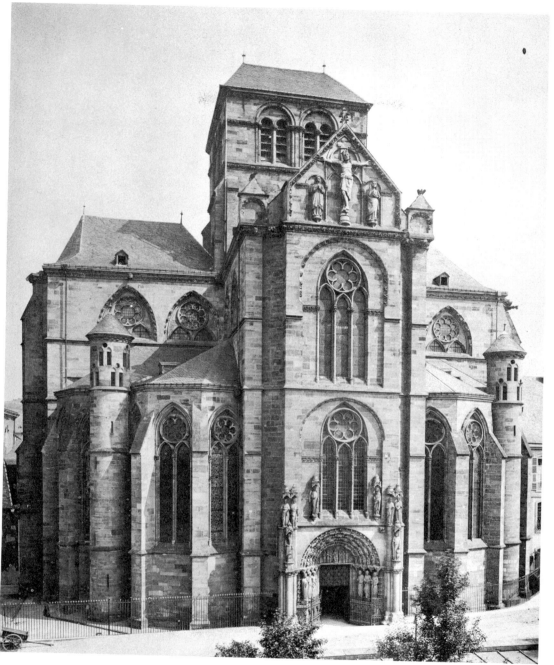

Liebfrauenkirche. Begun c. 1240. Trier, Germany. P: SBB

Interior and plan, Liebfrauenkirche. P: SBB

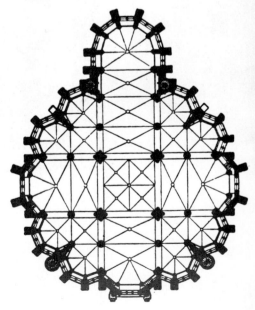

Choir. 1361–72. St. Sebald, Nuremberg, Germany. P: SBB

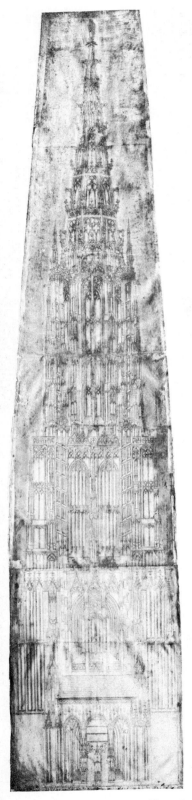

(A) Matthäus Böblinger. *Drawing for the Tower of the Ulm Münster.* 1482. Münsterbauamt, Ulm, Germany

(B) Münster, Ulm. (Upper part of tower late 19th century.) P: SBB

(A) St. Maclou. Begun 1434. Rouen. P: GIRAUDON

(B) The Cloth Hall.
Begun 1425.
Ghent, Belgium.
P: MARBURG

House of the silversmith and merchant Jacques Coeur.
1443–51. Bourges, France. P: ARCH. PHOT.

Choir. 1332–77. Gloucester Cathedral, England. P: KERSTING

Interior, King's College Chapel. 1446–1515. Cambridge,
England. P: KERSTING

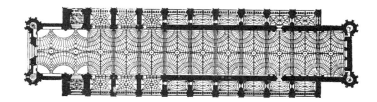

Exterior and Plan,
King's College Chapel.
Cambridge.
P: EDWIN SMITH

Chapel of Henry VII. 1503–19. Westminster Abbey,
London. P: KERSTING

Façade (detail). 1488–96. S. Gregorio, Valladolid,
Spain. P: MAS

Jamb Statues, West Portals. c. 1145–70. Chartres Cathedral.

Jamb Statues, South Transept Portals. c. 1215–20.
Chartres Cathedral. P: ROUBIER

(A) *Coronation of the Virgin*, tympanum of the center portal. c. 1190.
Notre Dame, Senlis, France. P: WARD

(B) *Death of the Virgin*, tympanum of the south-transept portal. c. 1220.
Strasbourg Cathedral, France. P: MARBURG

(A) *Vierge Dorée* (south-transept portal). c. 1250. Amiens Cathedral.

P: MARBURG

(B) *Le Beau Dieu* (center portal of the west façade). c. 1220–30. Amiens Cathedral. P: ROUBIER

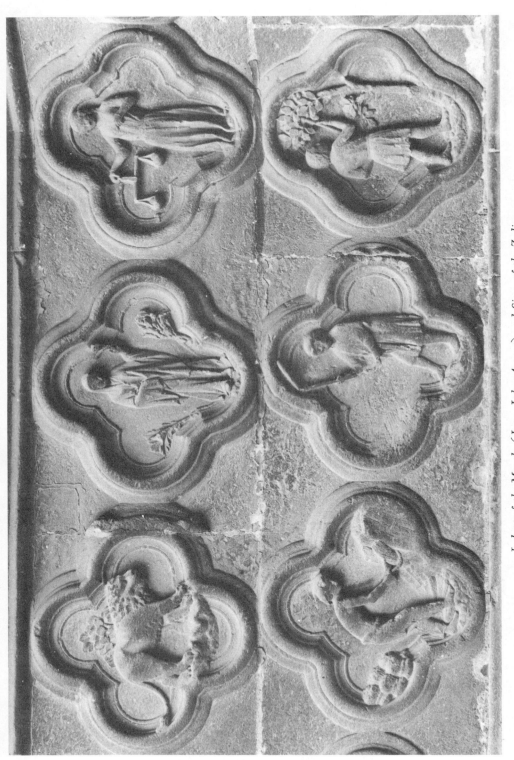

Labors of the Months (June, July, August) and Signs of the Zodiac (quatrefoil reliefs on the west façade). c. 1220–30. Amiens Cathedral. P: ROUBIER

Tomb of a Knight. c. 1230–50. Dorchester Abbey, Oxfordshire, England.

P: J. W. THOMAS, OXFORD

Tomb of Duke Henry the Lion and His Wife Mathilde. c. 1230–50.
Brunswick Cathedral, Germany. P: STADTBILDSTELLE, BRUNSWICK

Last Judgment Portal (north transept). c. 1220. Reims Cathedral.

P: ARCH. PHOT.

Annunciation and *Visitation* (west façade). c. 1225–35.
Reims Cathedral. P: ROUBIER

Detail of p. 486. P: ROUBIER

(A) *Elizabeth*. c. 1230–40.
Bamberg Cathedral. Germany.

P: SBB

(B) *Equestrian Figure of a King.*
c. 1230–40. Bamberg Cathedral.

P: WALTER HEGE, DTSCH. KUNSTVERL.

Ekkehard and Uta. c. 1250–60. Naumburg Cathedral, Germany.

P: SCHMIDT-GLASSNER

Crucifixion (choir screen). c. 1250–60. Naumburg Cathedral.

P: SBB

Abraham and Melchizedek (interior west wall). After 1251.
Reims Cathedral. P: MARBURG

(A) *Virgin and Child (Vierge de Paris).*
Early 14th century.
Notre Dame, Paris. P: MARBURG

(B) *Tomb of Bishop Friedrich von Hohenlohe.*
1351. Bamberg Cathedral.
P: WALTER HEGE, DTSCH. KUNSTVERL.

Pietà. Early 14th century. Wood, 34½″. Provinzialmuseum, Bonn.

Crucifix (Pestkreuz).
1304. Wood, 57″.
St. Marie im
Kapitol, Cologne.
P: RHEINISCHES
BILDARCHIV,
COLOGNE

King Charles V and *Jeanne de Bourbon*, from the Portal of the Celestine Monastery, Paris. c. 1375. 77″. The Louvre, Paris. P: ARCH. PHOT.

JEAN DE MARVILLE and CLAUS SLUTER. Portal of the Chartreuse de Champmol.
1385–93. Dijon, France. P: ARCH. PHOT.

OPPOSITE PAGE
CLAUS SLUTER. The Moses Well. 1395–1406. Figures c. 72″.
Chartreuse de Champmol, Dijon. P: ARCH. PHOT.

(A) CLAUS SLUTER and CLAUS DE WERWE.
Mourning Monk, from the Tomb of
Philip the Bold. Completed 1411. c. 16″.
Museum, Dijon. P: RIJKSMUSEUM, AMSTERDAM

(B) *Madonna*, from Krumau.
c. 1400–20. 43″.
Kunsthistorisches Museum, Vienna

(B) NICHOLAS OF VERDUN. *The Three Marys at the Tomb* (sketch engraved on the back of one of the enamel plaques of the altar). Klosterneuburg Abbey. P: BUNDESAMT FÜR DENKMALSPFLEGE, VIENNA

(A) NICHOLAS OF VERDUN. *The Crossing of the Red Sea* (enamel plaque of the altar). 1181. 5½″. Klosterneuburg Abbey, Austria.

P: BUNDESAMT FÜR DENKMALSPFLEGE, VIENNA

Illuminated Page (I Kings 11:2), from the *Psalter of St. Louis.*
c. 1260. Bibliothèque Nationale, Paris

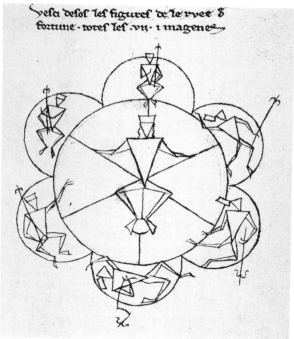

(A, B) VILLARD DE HONNECOURT. *Lion* ("drawn from life") and *Wheel of Fortune*, from sketchbook. c. 1240. Bibliothèque Nationale, Paris

(C) MASTER HONORÉ? *David and Goliath*, from the *Prayer Book of Philip the Fair*. 1295. Bibliothèque Nationale, Paris

JEAN PUCELLE. *The Presentation in the Temple* and *The Crucifixion*, from
The Hours of Jeanne d'Evreux. 1325–28. Slightly enlarged. Metropolitan Museum of Art,
New York (The Cloisters Collection. Purchase, 1954)

Scenes from the Passion of Christ, with Portraits of Charles V of France and His Queen,
from the *Parement de Narbonne.* c. 1375. Brush drawing in grisaille on a
white silk hanging, 30½ x 112½". The Louvre, Paris. P: GIRAUDON

Scenes of Country Life (detail). c. 1345. Fresco.
Palace of the Popes, Avignon. P: ARCH. PHOT.

BOHEMIAN SCHOOL. *Death of the Virgin.* c. 1360. Panel,
39 x 27¾". Museum of Fine Arts, Boston

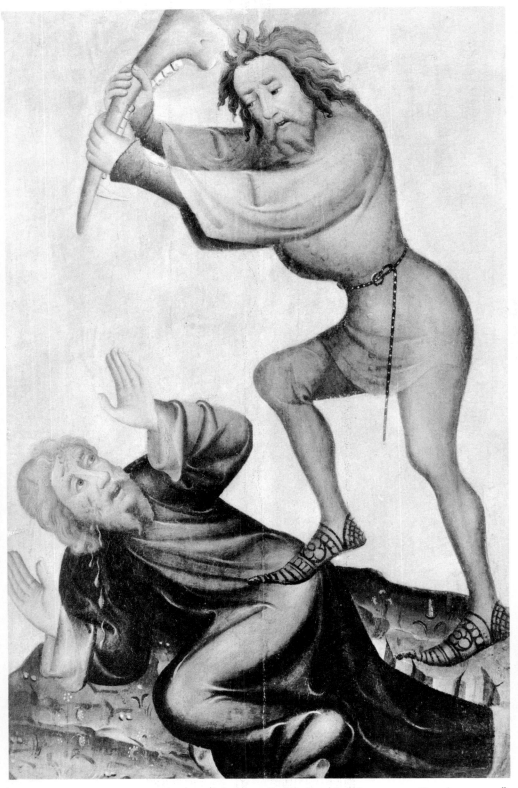

MASTER BERTRAM. *Cain Slaying Abel*, from the St. Peter's Altar. 1379. Panel, 32 x 20″.
Kunsthalle, Hamburg. P: KLEINHEMPEL, HAMBURG

King John the Good of France. c. 1360. Panel, 26 x 17¼".
The Louvre, Paris. P: BULLOZ

Melchior Broederlam. *The Presentation in the Temple and the Flight into Egypt.*
1394–99. Panel (altar shutter), 64 x 51″. Museum, Dijon

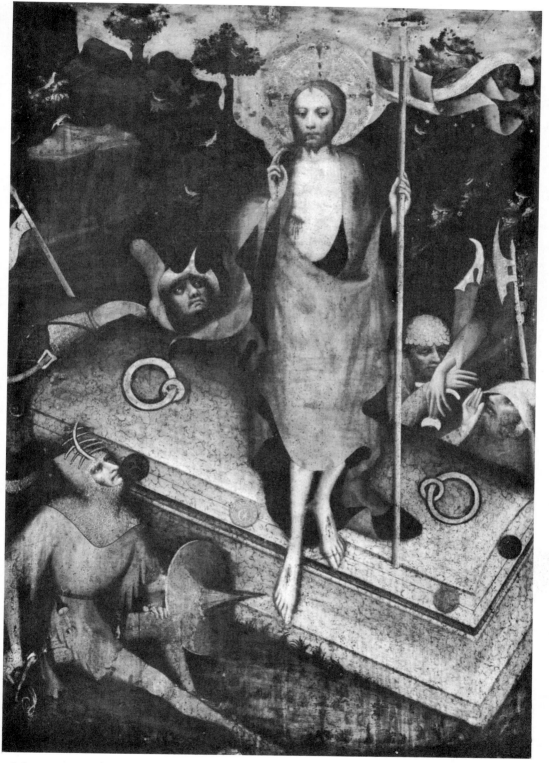

MASTER OF THE TREBON (WITTINGAU) ALTAR. *The Resurrection.* c. 1380–90. Panel, 52 x 36″.
National Gallery, Prague

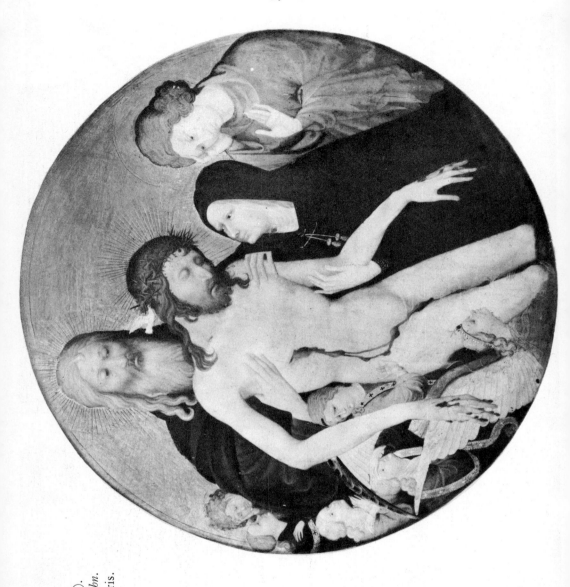

RIGHT

JEAN MALOUEL (or HENRI BELLECHOSE?).
The Holy Trinity with the Virgin and St. John.
C. 1400–10. Panel, 25¼″. The Louvre, Paris.
P: ARCH. PHOT.

OPPOSITE PAGE

Richard II Presented to the Madonna
(The "Wilton Diptych"). C. 1415.
Panel, each 18 x 11½″.
National Gallery, London

MASTER OF HEILIGENKREUZ. *The Annunciation*. C. 1400. Panel, 28 x 17″.
Kunsthistorisches Museum, Vienna

The Visitation, from the *Hours of the Maréchal de Boucicaut.*
c. 1410. Jacquemart-André Museum, Paris. P: BULLOZ

THE LIMBOURG BROTHERS. *January*, from *Les très riches heures du duc de Berry.*
1413–16. Condé Museum, Chantilly, France. P: GIRAUDON

THE LIMBOURG BROTHERS. *February,* from *Les très riches heures du duc de Berry.*
P: GIRAUDON

THE LIMBOURG BROTHERS. *October,* from *Les très riches heures du duc de Berry.*
P: GIRAUDON

THE MIDDLE AGES

16. Gothic Art in Italy

ANDREA PISANO. *The Creation of Adam* (marble relief on the Campanile). c. 1335–40.
Florence Cathedral. P: ALINARI

Church of Fossanova Abbey. Consecrated 1208. Near Piperno.

P: FOT. UNIONE

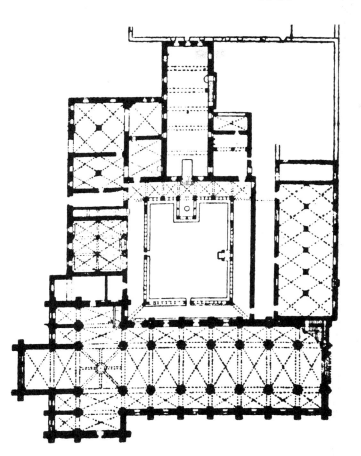

Nave of church and plan of Abbey. Fossanova.
P: H. W. JANSON

Florence Cathedral. Begun by Arnolfo di Cambio, 1296.
Dome by Filippo Brunelleschi, 1420–36. P: ALINARI

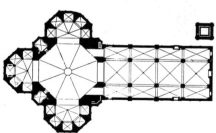

ABOVE AND RIGHT
(A, B) Interior and plan,
Florence Cathedral.

P: ALINARI

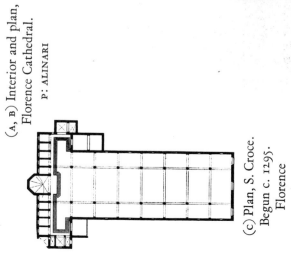

(c) Plan, S. Croce.
Begun c. 1295.
Florence

Interior, S. Croce. Florence. P: ARNOLD V. BORSIG, NEW YORK

Façade. c. 1310. Orvieto Cathedral. P: ANDERSON

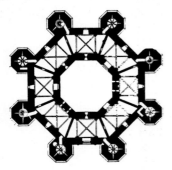

View and plan of Castel del Monte. c. 1240. Apulia.
P: HANS DECKER, FROM *Romanesque Art in Italy*

Palazzo Vecchio. Begun 1298. Florence. P: ALINARI

RIGHT
Ca' d'Oro. 1422–c. 1440.
Venice. P: ALINARI

OPPOSITE PAGE
Milan Cathedral. Begun 1386.
P: FOT. UNIONE

Interior, Milan Cathedral. P: ALINARI

NICOLA PISANO. Marble Pulpit. 1259–60.
Baptistery, Pisa. P: BROGI

Nativity, detail of
the Marble Pulpit.
Baptistery, Pisa
(see p. 529). P: BROGI

Giovanni Pisano.
Nativity, detail of the
Marble Pulpit. 1302–10.
Pisa Cathedral. p: alinari

GIOVANNI PISANO. *Strength and Prudence*, detail of the Marble Pulpit.
Pisa Cathedral. P: ALINARI

GIOVANNI PISANO. *Madonna*. c. 1315. Marble, 27″.
Prato Cathedral. P: BARSOTTI, FLORENCE

ARNOLFO DI CAMBIO.
Virgin and Child, from the
façade of Florence Cathedral.
c. 1300. Marble, 68½".
Cathedral Museum, Florence.
P: SOPR. GALL. FLOR.

LORENZO MAITANI. *The Last Judgment* (detail). c. 1320. Façade, Orvieto Cathedral.

P: RAFFAELLI, ARMONI & MORETTI, ORVIETO

Lorenzo Ghiberti. *The Sacrifice of Isaac.* 1401-2. Gilt bronze, 21 x 17½"
(without the molding). National Museum, Florence. P: ANDERSON

LORENZO GHIBERTI. *The Expulsion of the Money-Changers*, detail of the north doors.
c. 1415. Bronze, 21 x 17½″ (without the molding).
Baptistery, Florence. P: BROGI

Jacobello and Pierpaolo dalle Masegne. *Apostles*, detail of the choir screen. 1394.
Marble, c. 53″ . St. Mark's, Venice. P: Alinari

NANNI DI BANCO. *Four Saints (Quattro Coronati).*
c. 1410–14. Marble, approximately lifesize.
Exterior Tabernacle, Or San Michele, Florence.

P: BROGI

PIETRO CAVALLINI. *The Last Judgment* (details). c. 1295. Fresco.
S. Cecilia in Trastevere, Rome. P: GFN

CIMABUE ? *Crucifix.* c. 1290. Panel, 16′4″ x 12′9″.
S. Croce, Florence. P: ALINARI

CIMABUE. *Madonna Enthroned*. c. 1280–90. Panel, 12′7½″ x 7′4″.
Uffizi Gallery, Florence. P: ANDERSON

GIOTTO. *Madonna Enthroned*. c. 1310. Panel, 10′8″ x 6′8″.
Uffizi Gallery, Florence. P: BROGI

GIOTTO. *Christ Entering Jerusalem.* 1305–6. Fresco.
Arena Chapel, Padua. P: ALINARI

GIOTTO. *The Lamentation.* 1305–6. Fresco.
Arena Chapel, Padua. P. ALINARI

GIOTTO. *The Death of St. Francis.* c. 1318–20. Fresco.
S. CROCE, Florence. P: ALINARI

Maso di Banco? *A Miracle of St. Sylvester.* c. 1340. Fresco.
S. Croce, Florence. p: ALINARI

ABOVE

Duccio. *Madonna Enthroned*, detail of the *Maestà Altar*.
1308–11. Panel, 82½". Cathedral Museum, Siena. P: ANDERSON

OPPOSITE PAGE

Duccio. *Christ Entering Jerusalem*, panel of the *Maestà Altar*. 1308–11. 40 x 21".
Cathedral Museum, Siena. P: ANDERSON

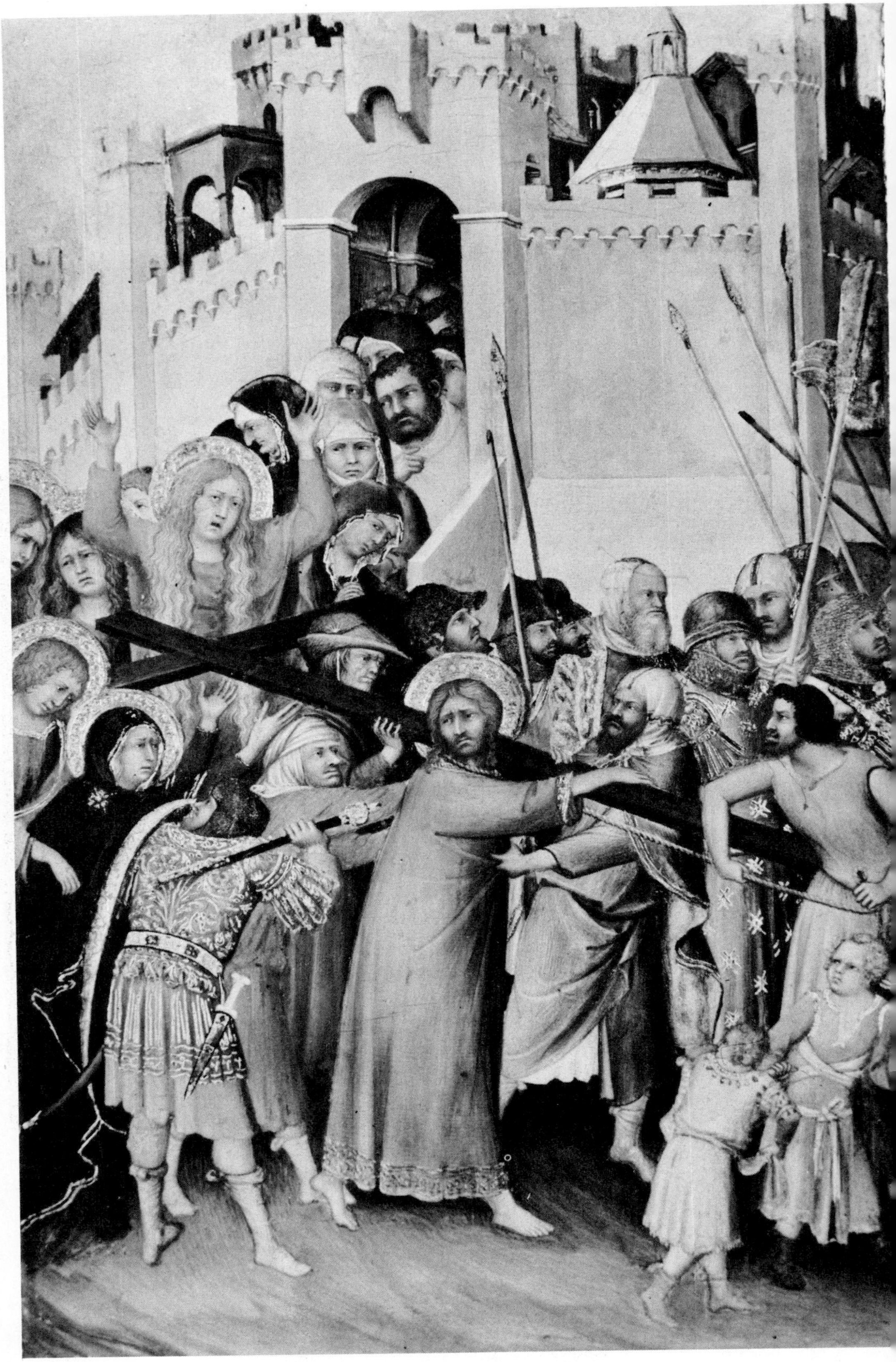

ABOVE
SIMONE MARTINI. *The Virgin*, detail of *The Annunciation*.
1333. Panel, 8′8″ x 10′ (this detail, c. 48 x 38″).
Uffizi Gallery, Florence. P: ALINARI

OPPOSITE PAGE
SIMONE MARTINI. *The Road to Calvary*. c. 1340. Panel, 11¾ x 8″.
The Louvre, Paris. P: ARCH. PHOT.

PIETRO LORENZETTI. *The Birth of the Virgin.* 1342. Panel, 73½ x 71½".
Cathedral Museum, Siena. P: ANDERSON

OPPOSITE PAGE
AMBROGIO LORENZETTI. *Madonna and Child.* c. 1330. Panel, 35½ x 17¾".
Cappella del Seminario Arcivescovile, Siena. P: ANDERSON

AMBROGIO LORENZETTI. *Good Government* (detail). 1338–40. Fresco.
Palazzo Pubblico, Siena. P: ANDERSON

Francesco Traini. *The Triumph of Death* (detail). c. 1350. Fresco. Camposanto, Pisa (destroyed 1944). P: ANDERSON

(A) AMBROGIO LORENZETTI. *Good Government* (detail). 1338–40. Fresco.
Palazzo Pubblico, Siena. P: JOSEPHINE POWELL, ROME

(B) ANDREA DA FIRENZE. *The Church Militant and Triumphant* (detail). 1365-68. Fresco.
Spanish Chapel, S. Maria Novella, Florence. P: ANDERSON

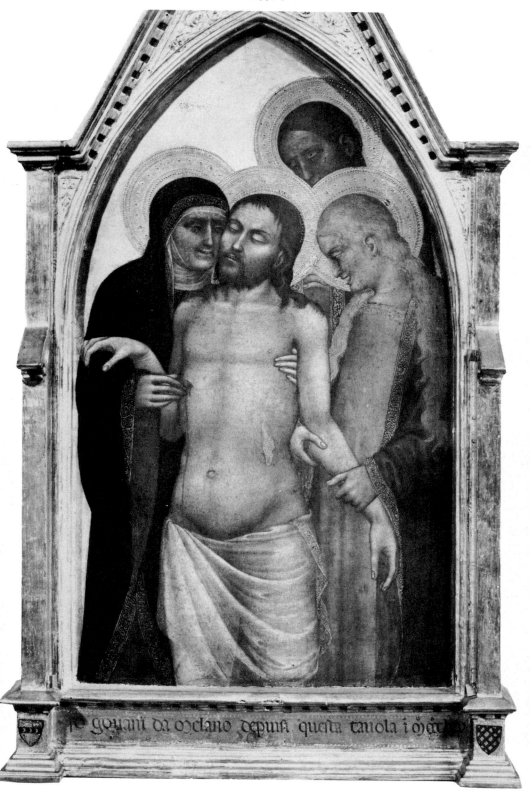

GIOVANNI DA MILANO. *The Lamentation*. 1365. Panel, 48 x 22¾".
Academy, Florence. P: SOPR. GALL. FLOR.

ALTICHIERO. *St. George Saved from the Wheel.* c. 1380–85. Fresco.
Oratorio di S. Giorgio, Padua. P: ALINARI

GENTILE DA FABRIANO. *The Adoration of the Magi* (altarpiece). 1423. Panel, 9′10″ x 9′3″.
Uffizi Gallery, Florence. P: ANDERSON

GENTILE DA FABRIANO. *The Nativity* (a predella panel of alterpiece on p. 559). 12¼ x 29½". P: ALINARI

LIST OF ILLUSTRATIONS

17. LATE GOTHIC ART NORTH OF THE ALPS

20. RENAISSANCE AND MANNERISM OUTSIDE ITALY

21. THE SEVENTEENTH CENTURY IN ITALY

22. THE SEVENTEENTH CENTURY IN FLANDERS, HOLLAND, AND GERMANY

23. THE SEVENTEENTH CENTURY IN FRANCE, ENGLAND, AND SPAIN

24. THE EIGHTEENTH CENTURY

THE RENAISSANCE

17. *Late Gothic Art*
North of the Alps

THE MASTER OF FLÉMALLE (ROBERT CAMPIN ?).
The Virgin and Child Before a Fire-Screen. C. 1425.
Panel, 25 x 19¼". National Gallery, London

e uentre matris mee uocauit me dñs
nomine meo. et posuit os meū sicut
gladium acutum sub tegumento
manus sue protexit me posuit me

HUBERT and/or JAN VAN EYCK. *The Birth of St. John* and *The Baptism of Christ*,
from the "Turin-Milan Hours." c. 1416–20. Museum, Turin. P: ACL

HUBERT and/or JAN VAN EYCK. *The Crucifixion* and *The Last Judgment*.
c. 1420. Panels transferred to canvas, each 22¼ x 7¾".
Metropolitan Museum of Art, New York (Fletcher Fund, 1933)

ROGER VAN DER WEYDEN.
The Descent from the Cross.
c. 1435. Panel, 86½ x 103".
The Prado, Madrid. P: MAS

HUBERT and JAN
VAN EYCK.
The Ghent Altarpiece
(open).
Completed 1432.
12′9″ x 17′1″.
St. Bavo, Ghent,
Belgium.
P: ACL

(A) *Adam and Eve*,
detail of p. 577. P: ACL

(B) *Singing Angels*,
detail of p. 577. P: ACL

The Ghent Alterpiece (closed). P: ACL

JAN VAN EYCK. *A Man in a Red Turban (Self-Portrait?)*. 1433.
Panel, 10¼ x 7½". National Gallery, London

JAN VAN EYCK. *Madonna with the Chancellor Rolin.* c. 1434.
Panel, 26 x 24½″. The Louvre, Paris. P: ACL

JAN VAN EYCK. *Giovanni Arnolfini and His Bride*. 1434.
Panel, 33 x 22½". National Gallery, London

DIERIC BOUTS. *The Last Supper.* c. 1465. Panel, 71 x 59".
St. Peter's, Louvain, Belgium. P: ACL

HUGO VAN DER GOES. *The Portinari Altarpiece* (open). c. 1476.
9'2½" x 20'20½". Uffizi Gallery, Florence. P. KENNEDY

Detail of p. 584. P: ANDERSON

HUGO VAN DER GOES. *The Death of the Virgin.* C. 1478–80.
Panel, 57¾ x 47½″. Museum, Bruges, Belgium. P: ACL

Geertgen tot Sint Jans. *The Birth of Christ*. c. 1490.
Panel, 13½ x 10″. National Gallery, London

(B) ROGER VAN DER WEYDEN. *Francesco d'Este.*
c. 1455. Panel, 11¾ x 8".
Metropolitan Museum of Art, New York

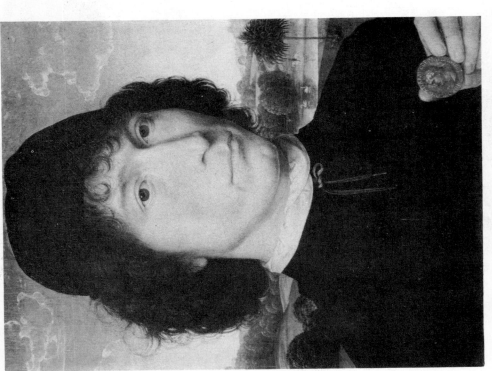

(A) HANS MEMLING. *Portrait of an Italian.*
c. 1485. Panel, 11½ x 8⅝".
Royal Museum of Fine Arts, Antwerp. P: ACL

HIERONYMUS BOSCH. *The Garden of Delights.* c. 1500. Central panel 86½ x 76¾", wings 86½ x 38". The Prado, Madrid. P: MAS

Detail of p. 589 (center panel). P: MAS

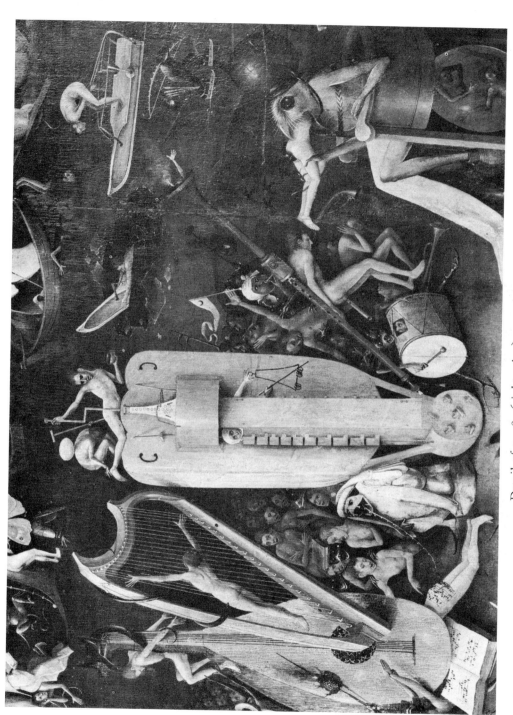

Detail of p. 589 (right wing). P: MAS

JEAN FOUQUET. *Etienne Chevalier and St. Stephen.* c. 1450.
Panel, 36½ x 33½". Formerly State Museums, Berlin

MASTER OF THE AIX ANNUNCIATION. *Jeremiah* (with the features of
King René d'Anjou). c. 1450. Panel, 60 x 34".
Royal Museums of Fine Arts, Brussels. P: ACL

OPPOSITE PAGE
SOUTHERN FRENCH MASTER.
The Avignon Pietà.
c. 1470. Panel, 64 x 86".
The Louvre, Paris.

P: GIRAUDON

CONRAD WITZ.
Christ Walking on the Water.
1444. Panel, 51 x 61".
Musée d'Art et d'Histoire,
Geneva

MICHAEL PACHER. *The Four Latin Fathers (Jerome, Augustine, Gregory, Ambrose).*
c. 1483. Center panel 81 x 77", wings 81 x 36½".
Pinakothek, Munich

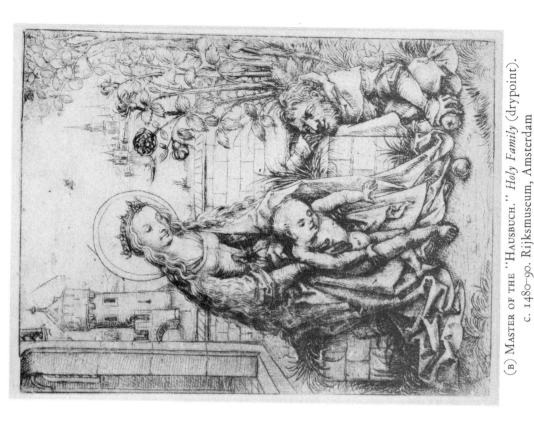

(B) Master of the "Hausbuch." *Holy Family* (drypoint).
c. 1480–90. Rijksmuseum, Amsterdam

(A) *St. Dorothy* (woodcut). c. 1420.
Staatliche Graphische Sammlung, Munich

MARTIN SCHONGAUER. *The Temptation of St. Anthony* (engraving). c. 1480–90.
Metropolitan Museum of Art, New York (Rogers Fund, 1920)

Nikolaus Gerhaert von Leyden. *Crucifix.* 1467. 90½″.
Cemetery, Baden-Baden, Germany. p: dtsch. kunstverl.

Flemish Master. Portrait Statuettes, from the Tomb of Isabella of Bourbon, Antwerp.
1476. Bronze, c. 22″. Rijksmuseum, Amsterdam

(B) Nikolaus Gerhaert von Leyden. *Grotesque Head*. c. 1465. 14″.
City Museum, Strasbourg. P: G. DETTLING, STRASBOURG

(A) Erasmus Grasser. *Morris Dancer*. 1480. Wood, c. 30″.
Historic City Museum, Munich. P: FRITZ THUDICHUM, MUNICH

BERNT NOTKE. *St. George and the Dragon.* 1483–89. Wood, c. 10′ x 13′9″.
St. Nicholas', Stockholm. P: REFOT, STOCKHOLM

VEIT STOSZ. *The Death of the Virgin.* 1477–89. Wooden shrine, 17½' wide, height of figures c. 9'. St. Mary's, Cracow. P: NATIONAL INSTITUTE OF ART HISTORY, WARSAW

MICHAEL PACHER. *Coronation of the Virgin* (center portion). 1471–81.
Wooden shrine, figures approximately lifesize.
Parish Church, St. Wolfgang, Austria. P: LÖBL, BAD TÖLZ

THE RENAISSANCE

18. The Early Renaissance in Italy

PISANELLO. *Emperor John Palaeologus VIII* (medal). 1438.
Bronze, diameter 4⅛". Victoria and Albert Museum, London

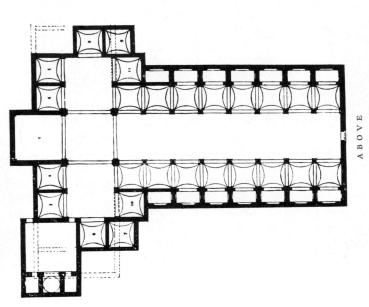

(A) Filippo Brunelleschi. Plan of S. Lorenzo.
1421–69. Florence

(B) Filippo Brunelleschi. The Old Sacristy.
1421–28. S. Lorenzo, Florence. (Sculptural
decoration by Donatello, c. 1430–43). P: ALINARI

Nave,
S. Lorenzo.
Florence.
P: ANDERSON

Filippo Brunelleschi. Exterior and interior view of the Pazzi Chapel. Begun 1430–33. S. Croce, Florence. p: anderson (ext.) and kidder smith (int.)

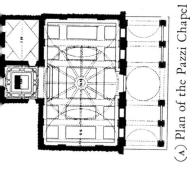

(A) Plan of the Pazzi Chapel

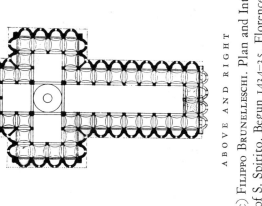

ABOVE AND RIGHT

(B, C) FILIPPO BRUNELLESCHI. Plan and Interior
of S. Spirito. Begun 1434–35. Florence.

MICHELOZZO. Palazzo Medici-Riccardi. Begun 1444.
Florence. P: ALINARI

LEONE BATTISTA ALBERTI. Palazzo Rucellai. 1446–51.
Florence. P: ANDERSON

LEONE BATTISTA ALBERTI.
Façade and plan of S. Andrea, Mantua.
P: ROLLIE MCKENNA, NEW YORK

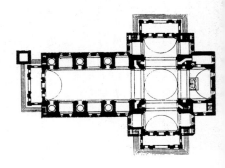

Mauro Coducci. Façade of S. Zaccaria. c. 1483–1500.
Venice. P: FIORENTINI

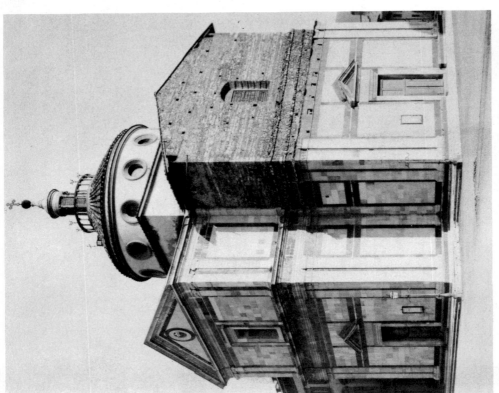

Giuliano da Sangallo. S. Maria delle Carceri.
1485-92. Prato. P: Alinari

DONATELLO. *St. George and the Dragon* (detail, see p. 618). 1417. Marble, 15¾".
Or San Michele, Florence. P: BROGI

DONATELLO.
St. George Tabernacle.
c. 1415–17. Marble
(the statue now replaced
by bronze copy),
height of statue
82″. Or San Michele,
Florence: P: ALINARI

DONATELLO. *St. Mark.*
1411–13. Marble, 93″.
Or San Michele,
Florence: P: BROGI

DONATELLO.
Prophet (Zuccone),
from the Campanile
of the Cathedral.
1423–25. Marble, 77″.
Cathedral Museum,
Florence. P: BROGI

JACOPO DELLA QUERCIA. *Acca Larentia with Romulus and Remus* (detail), from the Fonte Gaia.
1409–19. Marble, approximately lifesize. Palazzo Pubblico, Siena.
P: BROGI, COURTESY CHARLES SEYMOUR, JR.

JACOPO DELLA QUERCIA. *The Creation of Adam.* c. 1430. Marble, 34½ x 27½".
Main Portal (1425–38), S. Petronio, Bologna.
P: BROGI, COURTESY CHARLES SEYMOUR, JR.

Donatello. *The Feast of Herod* (detail of baptismal font). c. 1425.
Gilt bronze, 23½″ square. S. Giovanni, Siena. P: ANDERSON

LORENZO GHIBERTI. *The Baptism of Christ* (detail of baptismal font). c. 1425.
Gilt bronze, 23½″ square. S. Giovanni, Siena. P: BROGI

LORENZO GHIBERTI. *Isaac, Jacob, and Esau*, detail of the east doors ("Gates of Paradise"). c. 1435. Gilt bronze, 31¼″ square. Baptistery, Florence. P: BROGI

MICHELOZZO and DONATELLO. Outdoor Pulpit. 1428–38. Marble, each relief 29 x 31". Prato Cathedral. P: ALINARI

DONATELLO. *Cantoria.* 1433–39. Marble, 10′ 17″ x 18′ 8″.
Cathedral Museum, Florence. P: ANDERSON

Donatello. *Equestrian Monument of Gattamelata*. 1445–50. Bronze, c. 11′ x 13′.
Piazza del Santo, Padua. P: BROGI

(A) DONATELLO. *David*.
c. 1430–32. Bronze, 62¼″.
National Museum, Florence.
P: BROGI

(B) DONATELLO.
St. Mary Magdalen.
c. 1454–55. Wood, 74″.
Baptistery, Florence.
P: BROGI ·

Detail of p. 629 B. P: BROGI

OPPOSITE PAGE
LUCA DELLA ROBBIA. *Singing Angels*, from the *Cantoria*. c. 1435. Marble, c. 38 x 24".
Cathedral Museum, Florence. P: BROGI

Luca della Robbia. *Madonna and Angels*, lunette from the Via d'Agnolo. c. 1460. Glazed terracotta, 63 x 87½". National Museum, Florence. P: BROGI

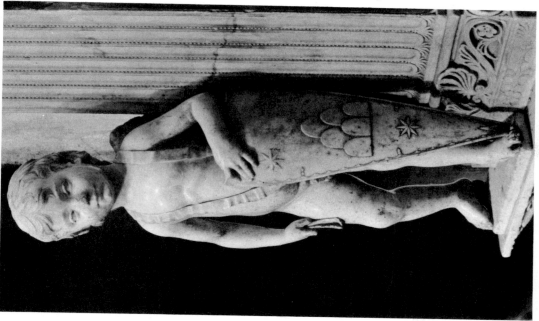

RIGHT

(A) DESIDERIO DA SETTIGNANO.
Putto, from the Tomb of
Carlo Marsuppini.
c. 1455. Marble, 38″.
S. Croce, Florence.

P: KENNEDY

FAR RIGHT

(B) ANDREA DEL VERROCCHIO.
Putto with Dolphin. c. 1470.
Bronze, 27″ (without base).
Palazzo Vecchio, Florence.

P: HILDE LOTZ, NEW YORK

ANTONIO ROSSELLINO. *Bust of Giovanni da San Miniato.* 1456. Marble, 20″.
Victoria and Albert Museum, London

BERNARDO ROSSELLINO. Tomb of Leonardo Bruni. c. 1445.
Marble, height (to top of arch) 20′. S. Croce, Florence. P: ALINARI

ANDREA DEL VERROCCHIO. *Equestrian Monument of Bartolommeo Colleoni.* 1485–88. Bronze, c. 13′.
Campo SS. Giovanni e Paolo, Venice. P: ANDERSON

ANDREA DEL VERROCCHIO. *Christ and the Doubting Thomas.* c. 1465–83.
Bronze, in marble tabernacle of c. 1423 by Donatello, height of niche 9′9″.
Or San Michele, Florence. P: BROGI

ANTONIO DEL POLLAIUOLO. *Hercules and Antaeus.* C. 1475. Bronze, 18″.
National Museum, Florence. P: ALINARI

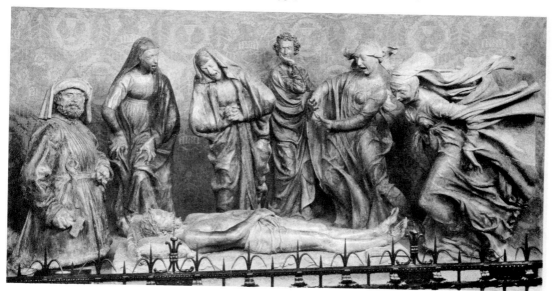

Niccolò dell'Arca. *The Lamentation*, and detail. c. 1485–90. Terracotta, approximately lifesize. S. Maria della Vita, Bologna. p: a. villani, bologna

MASACCIO.
*The Holy Trinity
with the Virgin
and St. John.*
c. 1425. Fresco.
S. Maria Novella,
Florence.
P: SOPR. GALL. FLOR.

MASACCIO. *The Tribute Money.* C. 1425. FRESCO.
Brancacci Chapel, S. Maria del Carmine, Florence. P: BROGI

MASACCIO.
Madonna and Child Enthroned.
1426. Panel, 56 x 29″.
National Gallery, London

BELOW

(A) MASACCIO.
The Expulsion from Paradise.
c. 1425. Fresco.
Brancacci Chapel,
S. Maria del Carmine,
Florence. P: ALINARI

ABOVE

(B) ANDREA DEL CASTAGNO.
David. c. 1450–55.
Leather, height 45½″, greatest width 30″.
National Gallery of Art,
Washington, D. C.
(Widener Collection)

(B) FRA FILIPPO LIPPI. *The Virgin Adoring the Child.*
c. 1460. Panel, 50 x 46".
Formerly State Museums, Berlin

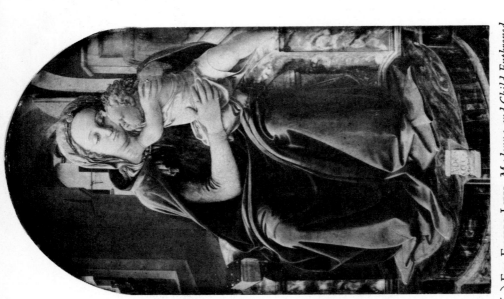

(A) FRA FILIPPO LIPPI. *Madonna and Child Enthroned.*
1437. Panel, 45 x 25½".
National Museum, Tarquinia. P: ALINARI

FRA ANGELICO. *The Annunciation.* c. 1445–50. Fresco.
S. Marco, Florence. P: ALINARI

Andrea del Castagno. *The Last Supper.* c. 1445–50. Fresco.
S. Apollonia, Florence. P: ANDERSON

PAOLO UCCELLO. *The Battle of San Romano*. c. 1455.
Panel, 72 x 125˝. National Gallery, London

Domenico Veneziano. *Madonna and Saints*. c. 1445. Panel, 79 x 84".
Uffizi Gallery, Florence. P: SOPR. GALL. FLOR.

Piero della Francesca. *The Resurrection*. c. 1460. Fresco (detached).
Picture Gallery, Borgo San Sepolcro. P: BROGI

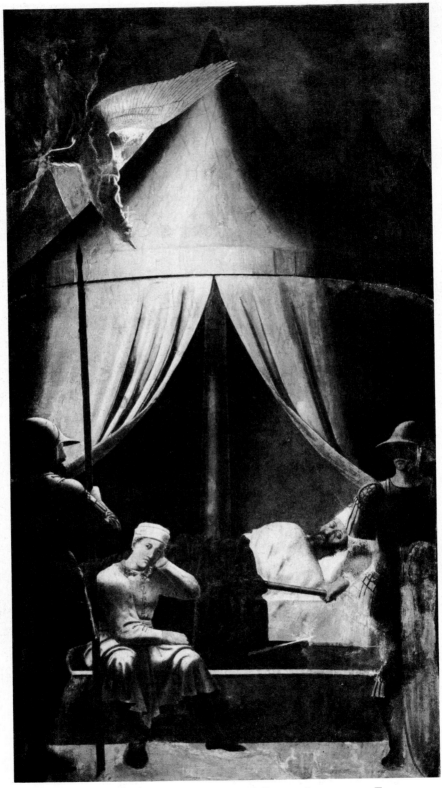

PIERO DELLA FRANCESCA. *The Dream of Constantine*. C. 1455. Fresco.
S. Francesco, Arezzo. P: ANDERSON

PIERO DELLA FRANCESCA. *The Discovery of the True Cross.* c. 1455. Fresco.
S. Francesco, Arezzo. P: ANDERSON

ANDREA MANTEGNA. *St. James Led to His Execution.* C. 1455. Fresco.
Ovetari Chapel, Church of the Eremitani, Padua (destroyed). P: ALINARI

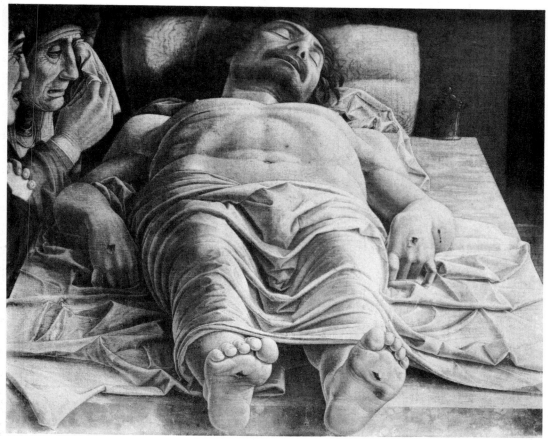

(A) ANDREA MANTEGNA. *The Lamentation*. c. 1490–1500.
Canvas, 27 x 32″. Brera Gallery, Milan. P: ALINARI

(B) ANDREA MANTEGNA.
The Entombment (engraving,
enlarged detail). c. 1475.
Metropolitan Museum
of Art, New York
(Dick Fund, 1937)

ANDREA MANTEGNA.
The Crucifixion.
1456–59. Panel,
26 x 35½".
The Louvre, Paris.
P: ARCH. PHOT.

ANDREA MANTEGNA.
Ceiling (portion).
c. 1470. Fresco.
Camera degli Sposi,
Ducal Palace, Mantua.

P: ANDERSON

ANTONELLO DA MESSINA. *The Crucifixion.* 1475. Panel, 23½ x 16¾".
Royal Museum of Fine Arts, Antwerp. P: ACL

Giovanni Bellini. *St. Francis in Ecstasy*. c. 1485. Panel, 48½ x 55".
The Frick Collection, New York

ABOVE

MELOZZO DA FORLÌ. *Sixtus IV and His Familiars.* c. 1475–77. Fresco (transferred to canvas), 12′2″ x 10′4″. Vatican Gallery, Rome. P: BROGI

OPPOSITE PAGE

GIOVANNI BELLINI. *Madonna and Saints.* 1505. Panel (transferred to canvas), 16′5½″ x 7′9″. S. Zaccaria, Venice. P: FIORENTINI

ANTONIO DEL POLLAIUOLO. *The Rape of Deianira.* c. 1475. Panel, 23½ x 31½".
Yale University Art Gallery, New Haven, Connecticut

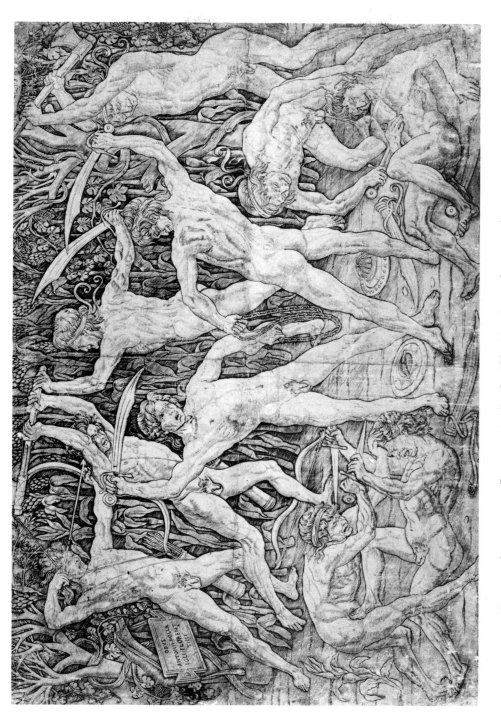

Antonio del Pollaiuolo. *Battle of Ten Naked Men* (engraving). c. 1465–70.
Metropolitan Museum of Art, New York (Joseph Pulitzer Bequest, 1917)

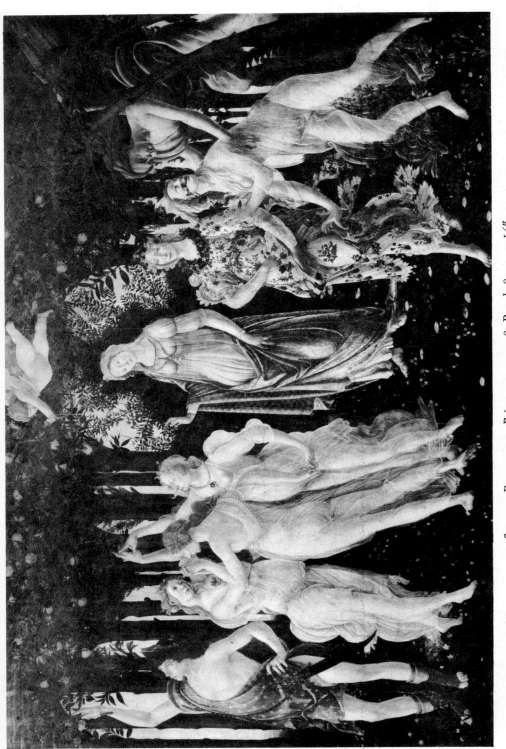

SANDRO BOTTICELLI. *Primavera.* c. 1478. Panel, 80 x 123½".
Uffizi Gallery, Florence

Sandro Botticelli. *The Birth of Venus.* c. 1480. Canvas, 79 x 110".
Uffizi Gallery, Florence. p: anderson

PIETRO PERUGINO. *The Delivery of the Keys*. 1482. Fresco.
Sistine Chapel, Vatican, Rome. P: ALINARI

DOMENICO GHIRLANDAIO. *The Birth of the Virgin.* 1486–90. Fresco.
S. Maria Novella, Florence. P: BROGI

OPPOSITE PAGE

PIERO DI COSIMO. *The Discovery of Honey.*
c. 1498. Panel, 31¼ x 50¼".
Worcester Art Museum, Massachusetts

RIGHT

LUCA SIGNORELLI.
The Damned Cast into Hell. c. 1500.
Fresco. S. Brizio Chapel,
Orvieto Cathedral. P: ALINARI

DOMENICO GHIRLANDAIO. *An Old Man and His Grandson.* c. 1480. Panel, 24½ x 18″.
The Louvre, Paris. P: ALINARI

THE RENAISSANCE

19. High Renaissance and Mannerism in Italy

BENVENUTO CELLINI. *The Saltcellar of Francis I.* 1539–43. Gold, 10¼ x 13⅛".
Kunsthistorisches Museum, Vienna

(A) Donato Bramante.
Dome and Choir.
Begun 1492.
S. Marie delle Grazie,
Milan.
P: ARAGOZZINI, MILAN

BELOW

(B) Leonardo da Vinci.
Project for a Church
(Ms. B). c. 1490.
Pen drawing.
Bibliothèque de l'Arsenal,
Paris. P: GIRAUDON

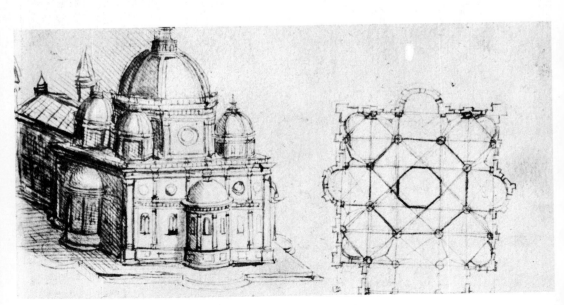

Interior, S. Maria delle Grazie, Milan. P: ARAGOZZINI, MILAN

Donato Bramante. Cloister. 1504. S. Maria della Pace, Rome. P. Anderson

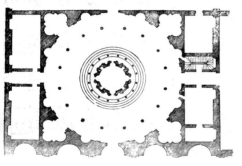

ABOVE

(A) DONATO BRAMANTE. The Tempietto.
1502. S. Pietro in Montorio,
Rome. P: GFN

LEFT

(B) Plan of the Tempietto, with
projected courtyard. (After Serlio)

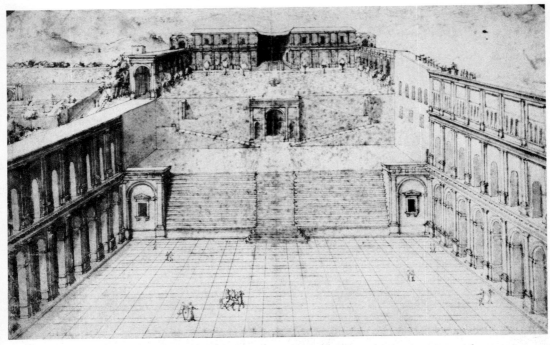

(A) *The Belvedere Court* (Vatican, Rome). Begun by Bramante c. 1503. After a 16th-century drawing in the collection of Edmonde Fatio, Geneva. P: SOPR. GALL. FLOR.

(B) CARADOSSO. Medal showing Bramante's design for St. Peter's, Rome. 1506. British Museum, London

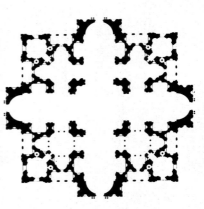

(C) DONATO BRAMANTE. Original plan for St. Peter's. 1506. (After Geymüller)

RIGHT
(D) RAPHAEL. Plan for St. Peter's, Rome. 1514–20. (After Serlio)

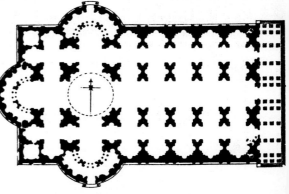

MICHELANGELO. Dome and plan of St. Peter's, Rome. 1558–60.
(Completed by Giacomo della Porta, 1590.) P: FOT. UNIONE

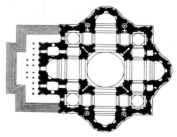

MICHELANGELO. Staircase of the Laurentian Library. 1524. Florence. P: ALINARI

GIULIO ROMANO. The Artist's House. c. 1544. Mantua. P: GFN

(A) MICHELANGELO. The Campidoglio. Designed 1537. Rome. P: KERSTING

(B) *The Campidoglio*, engraving by Etienne Dupérac. 1569.
Gabinetto Nazionale delle Stampe, Rome

ANTONIO DA SANGALLO and MICHELANGELO. Façade and courtyard of the Palazzo Farnese. 1530–48. Rome. P: ALINARI (ABOVE) AND ANDERSON

(A) BALDASSARE PERUZZI. Palazzo Massimi. Begun 1535. Rome. P: ALINARI

(B) VASARI, VIGNOLA, and AMMANATI. Villa Giulia. 1550-55. Rome. P: ALINARI

(A) GIORGIO VASARI. Loggia of the Uffizi (view from the Arno).
Begun 1560. Florence. P: BROGI

(B) BARTOLOMMEO AMMANATI. Courtyard of the Palazzo Pitti.
1558–70. Florence. P: ANDERSON

Loggia of the Uffizi (view toward the Arno; see p. 681 A).
P: HILDE LOTZ, NEW YORK

JACOPO SANSOVINO. The Library of St. Mark's. Begun 1536.
Venice. P: ANDERSON

Andrea Palladio. Villa Rotonda. Begun 1550. Vicenza. p: rollie mc kenna, new york

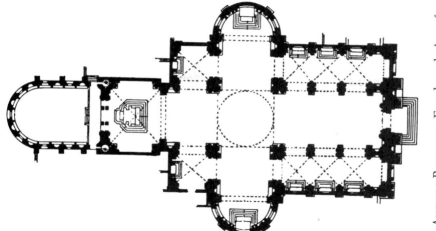

Andrea Palladio. Façade and plan of
S. Giorgio Maggiore. Designed 1565.
Venice. p: fond. cini

Interior, S. Giorgio Maggiore. Venice. P: FOND. CINI

Andrea Palladio. The Teatro Olimpico. 1580–84. Vicenza. p: Kidder Smith

MICHELANGELO. *David.*
1501–4. Marble, 18′.
Academy, Florence.
P: ANDERSON

MICHELANGELO. *Moses.* C. 1513–15. Marble, 8′4″.
S. Pietro in Vincoli, Rome. P: MARBURG

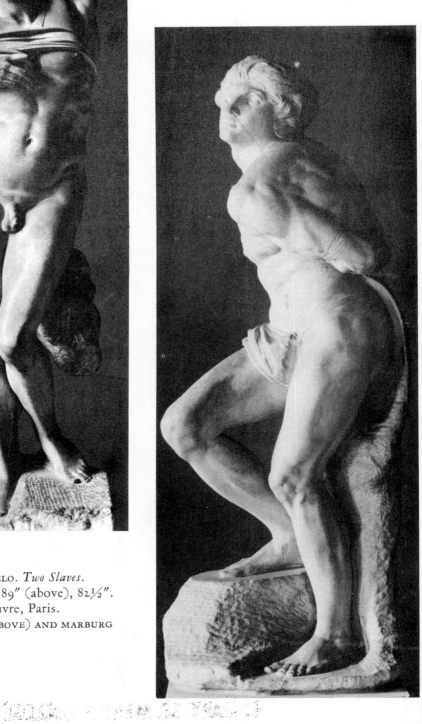

MICHELANGELO. *Two Slaves.*
1513–16. Marble, 89″ (above), 82½″.
The Louvre, Paris.
P: ARCH. PHOT. (ABOVE) AND MARBURG

MICHELANGELO. Tomb of Giuliano de'Medici. 1524–34. Marble,
height of central figure 71″. New Sacristy,
S. Lorenzo, Florence. P: ALINARI

MICHELANGELO. *The Medici Madonna.* 1521–34. Marble, 81½″.
New Sacristy, S. Lorenzo, Florence. P: BROGI

MICHELANGELO. *Pietà Rondanini*. c. 1555–64. Marble, 77½″.
Castello Sforzesco, Milan

BELOW

(A) BENVENUTO CELLINI.
Perseus. 1545–54.
Bronze, 10′6″ (without the base).
Loggia dei Lanzi, Florence.
P: ALINARI

ABOVE

(B) *Jupiter* (detail of base).
P: ALINARI

OPPOSITE PAGE

GIOVANNI DA BOLOGNA. *Mercury.* Completed 1580.
Bronze, 69″. National Museum, Florence.
P: ANDERSON

GIOVANNI DA BOLOGNA. *The Rape of the Sabine Woman*. Completed 1583.
Marble, 13′6″. Loggia dei Lanzi, Florence. P: BROGI (LEFT) AND ALINARI

OPPOSITE PAGE
LEONARDO DA VINCI. *The Virgin of the Rocks*. C. 1485.
Panel, 75 x 43½″. The Louvre, Paris. P: GIRAUDON

LEONARDO DA VINCI. *Adoration of the Magi* (detail). 1481–82. Panel, size of the area shown c. 24 × 30″. Uffizi Gallery, Florence. P: ALINARI

LEONARDO DA VINCI. *The Last Supper*. c. 1495–98. Fresco.
S. Maria delle Grazie, Milan. P: BRERA GALLERY, MILAN

LEONARDO DA VINCI. *St. Anne with the Virgin and Child
and the Infant St. John* (cartoon). 1498–1500. 54¾ x 39¾".
Burlington House, London

LEONARDO DA VINCI. *Mona Lisa.* c. 1503–5. Panel, 30¼ x 21″.
The Louvre, Paris. P: ALINARI

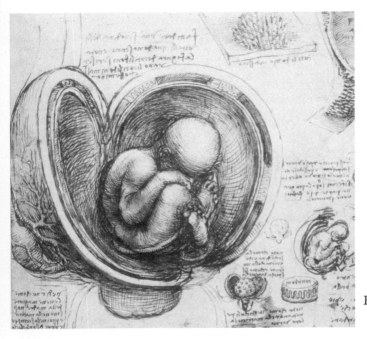

(A) LEONARDO DA VINCI.
Embryo in the Womb.
c. 1510. Pen drawing.
Royal Library, Windsor Castle.
(Crown copyright reserved)

(B) LEONARDO DA VINCI. *Coastal Landscape in a Storm.* c. 1510. Pen and chalk drawing.
Royal Library, Windsor Castle. (Crown copyright reserved)

Interior of the Sistine Chapel
(showing Michelangelo's Ceiling Fresco and *Last Judgment*).
Vatican, Rome. P: ANDERSON

MICHELANGELO. *The Creation of Adam*, detail of the ceiling. 1508–12. Sistine Chapel. P: ANDERSON

MICHELANGELO. *The Lord Dividing Light from Darkness*,
detail of the ceiling. 1508–12. Sistine Chapel. P: ANDERSON

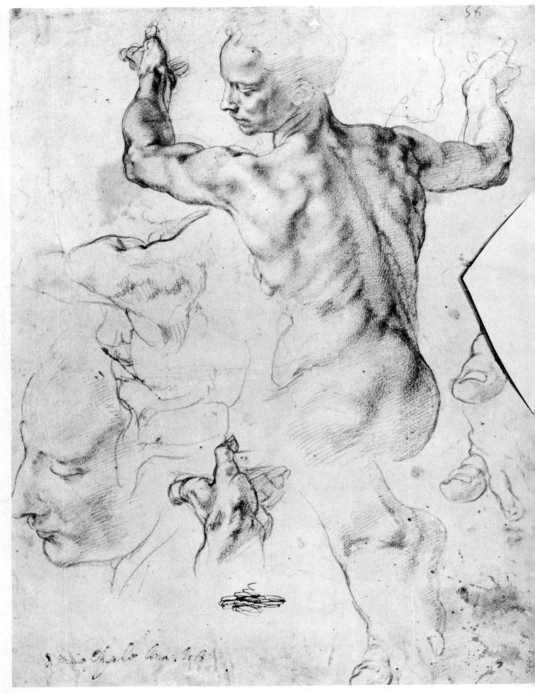

MICHELANGELO. *Study for the Libyan Sibyl.* c. 1510. Red chalk drawing.
Metropolitan Museum of Art, New York (Joseph Pulitzer Fund, 1924)

MICHELANGELO. Detail from the *Last Judgment* (with self-portrait). 1534–41. Sistine Chapel. P: ANDERSON

ABOVE

(A) RAPHAEL. *Head of a Youth.* C. 1497–1504.
Black chalk drawing. Ashmolean Museum, Oxford

RIGHT

(B) RAPHAEL. *Portrait of a Cardinal.* C. 1510.
Panel, 31 x 24″. The Prado, Madrid. P: ANDERSON

RAPHAEL. *The School of Athens.* 1509–10. Fresco.
Stanza della Segnatura, Vatican, Rome. P: BROGI

RAPHAEL. *Madonna del Granduca.* c. 1505. Panel, 33 x 21½".
Pitti Palace, Florence. P: ALINARI

RAPHAEL. *Galatea*. c. 1514. Fresco.
Villa Farnesina, Rome. P: ALINARI

Il Rosso Fiorentino. *The Descent from the Cross.* 1521. Panel, 11' x 6'5½".
Picture Gallery, Volterra. p: sopr. gall. flor.

PONTORMO. *The Entombment.* 1525–28. Panel, 123 x 75½″.
S. Felicità, Florence. P: SOPR. GALL. FLOR.

OPPOSITE PAGE
PONTORMO.
Study of a Young Girl.
c. 1526. Sanguine drawing.
Uffizi Gallery, Florence.
P: SOPR. GALL. FLOR.

ABOVE
(A) PARMIGIANINO.
Self-Portrait. 1524.
Panel, diameter 9⅝".
Kunsthistorisches Museum,
Vienna.
P: F. BRUCKMANN, MUNICH

LEFT
(B) UGO DA CARPI,
after PARMIGIANINO.
Diogenes.
c. 1523–27.
Chiaroscuro woodcut.
Private collection

ABOVE
GIORGIONE. *The Tempest.* c. 1505. 32¼ x 28¾".
Academy, Venice. P: FIORENTINI

OPPOSITE PAGE
PARMIGIANINO. *Madonna with the Long Neck.* c. 1535. Panel, 85 x 52".
Uffizi Gallery, Florence. P: ANDERSON

TITIAN. *Madonna with Members of the Pesaro Family.* 1526. 16′ x 8′10″.
Church of the Frari, Venice. P: ANDERSON

TITIAN. *Bacchus and Ariadne.*
c. 1520. 69 x 75".
National Gallery, London

TITIAN. *Man with the Glove.* c. 1520. 39½ x 35".
The Louvre, Paris: P: ALINARI

TITIAN. *Paul III and His Grandsons.* 1546. 78½ x 49″.
National Museum, Naples. P: BROGI

TITIAN. *Christ Crowned with Thorns.* c. 1565.
110 x 72". Pinakothek, Munich

CORREGGIO. *The Holy Night.* 1522–30. 100½ x 74".
State Picture Gallery, Dresden. P: ALINARI

CORREGGIO. *The Assumption of the Virgin* (detail). c. 1525.
Fresco. Dome, Parma Cathedral. P: ANDERSON

CORREGGIO.
Jupiter and Io.
c. 1532.
64½ x 27¾".
Kunsthistorisches
Museum, Vienna

TINTORETTO.
The Finding of the Body of St. Mark.
c. 1562. 13′ 3½″ square.
Brera Gallery, Milan

TINTORETTO. *The Last Supper.*
1592–94. 12′ x 18′8″.
S. Giorgio Maggiore, Venice.
P: FOND. CINI

PAOLO VERONESE. Ceiling Fresco. c. 1567.
Villa Giacomelli, Masèr. P: ALINARI

Paolo Veronese. *Christ in the House of Levi*, and detail. 1573. 18′2″ x 42′.
Academy, Venice. P: ANDERSON (ABOVE) AND FIORENTINI

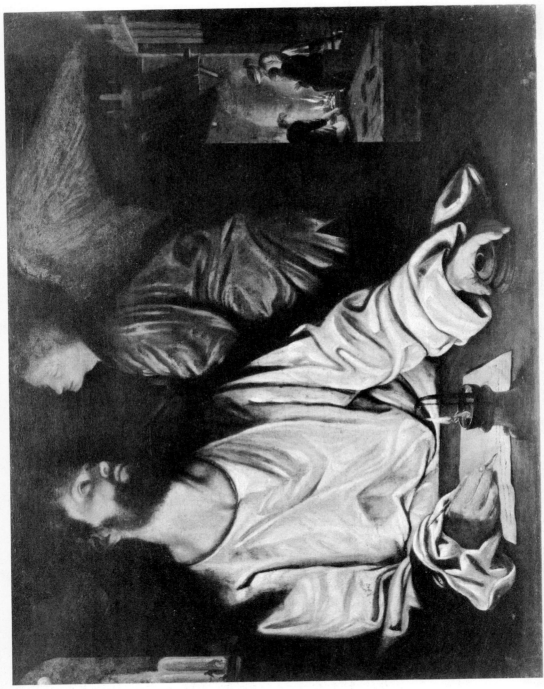

GIROLAMO SAVOLDO.
St. Matthew. c. 1535.
36¾ x 49″.
Metropolitan Museum
of Art, New York
(Marquand Fund, 1912)

GIAMBATTISTA MORONI. *A Tailor.* c. 1570.
38½ x 29½". National Gallery, London

AGNOLO BRONZINO. *Eleonora of Toledo and Her Son Giovanni de' Medici.* c. 1550. 45¼ x 37¾".
Uffizi Gallery, Florence. P: BROGI

THE RENAISSANCE

20. *Renaissance and Mannerism outside Italy*

Nicholas Hilliard. *A Young Man Among Roses*. c. 1588. Miniature
on parchment, 5⅜ x 2¾". Victoria and Albert Museum, London

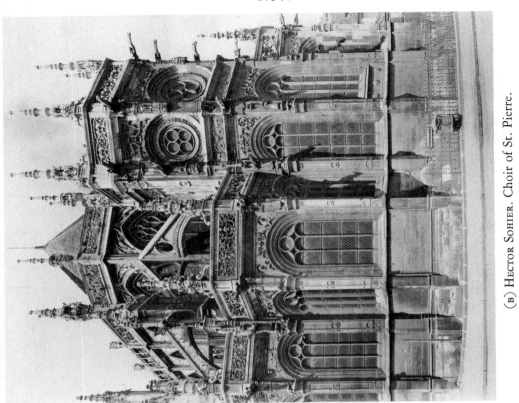

(B) HECTOR SOHIER. Choir of St. Pierre. 1528–45. Caen. P: MARBURG

(A) PIERRE LESCOT. The Fountain of the Innocents. 1547–49. Paris. P: GIRAUDON

(A) Aerial view of the Louvre, Paris. P: COMPAGNIE AÉRIENNE FRANÇAISE, SURESNES

RIGHT

(B) PHILIBERT DE L'ORME. Frontispiece from the Château of Anet. Before 1550. Ecole des Beaux-Arts, Paris. P: COURTAULD INST.

The Château of Chambord (north front). Begun 1519.
France. P: ARCH. PHOT.

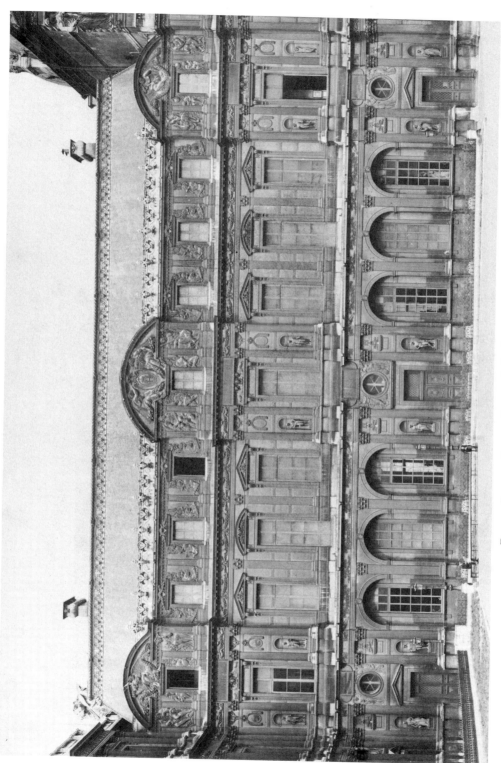

Pierre Lescot. Square Court of the Louvre. Begun 1546.
Paris. P: Giraudon

PETER VISCHER THE ELDER. *King Arthur.* 1513.
Bronze, lifesize. Hofkirche, Innsbruck, Austria.

Francesco Primaticcio. Stucco Decoration. c. 1541–45.
Fontainebleau. p: courtesy editions "tel," paris

Jean Goujon. Nymphs, Fountain of the Innocents
(after plaster casts). 1548–49. Approximately lifesize
(see p. 734 A). P: BULLOZ

FRENCH FOLLOWER OF PRIMATICCIO.
Diana, from the Château of Anet.
Before 1554. Marble, 61 x 98½".
The Louvre, Paris. P: ALINARI

LEFT

(A) FRANCESCO PRIMATICCIO
and GERMAIN PILON.
Tomb of Henry II.
Begun 1563. Abbey Church
of St. Denis, Paris.
P: GIRAUDON

BELOW

(B) GERMAIN PILON.
*Gisants of the King
and Queen*, detail of
the Tomb of Henry II.
P: ARCH. PHOT.

ALONSO BERRUGUETE. *St. John the Baptist* (detail of choir stall). c. 1540.
Wood, 31½ x 19¼". Toledo Cathedral, Spain. P: MAS

MATTHIAS GRÜNEWALD.
The Crucifixion,
outer wings of the *Isenheim Altar.*
1509–11. Panel, 8′10″ x 10′1″.
Unterlinden Museum,
Colmar, France.

P: F. BRUCKMANN, MUNICH

OPPOSITE PAGE
ALBRECHT DÜRER. *Alpine Landscape.*
c. 1495. Watercolor.
Ashmolean Museum, Oxford

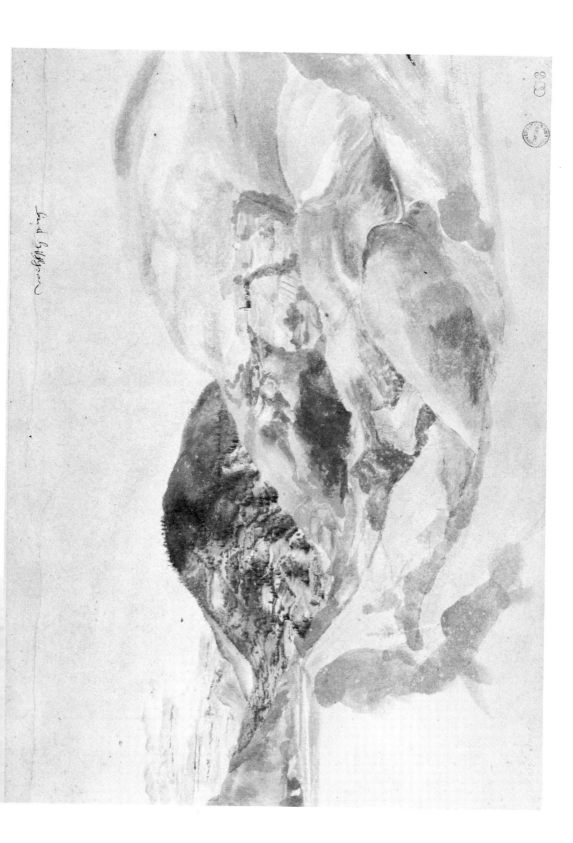

ALBRECHT DÜRER. *The Four Horsemen of the Apocalypse.* c. 1497–98. Woodcut.
Metropolitan Museum of Art, New York (Gift of Junius S. Morgan, 1919)

(A) ALBRECHT DÜRER.
Self-Portrait. 1484.
Silverpoint.
Albertina, Vienna

(B) ALBRECHT DÜRER.
*Demonstration of
Perspective Drawing of
a Lute,* from the 1525
edition of the artist's
treatise on geometry. Woodcut.
Metropolitan Museum of Art,
New York (Dick Fund, 1941)

ALBRECHT DÜRER. *Self-Portrait*. 1500. Panel, 26¼ x 19¼".
Pinakothek, Munich

ALBRECHT DÜRER. *Adam and Eve.* 1504. Engraving.
Museum of Fine Arts, Boston

ALBRECHT DÜRER. *Knight, Death, and Devil.*
1513. Engraving. Museum of Fine Arts, Boston

ALBRECHT DÜRER. *The Four Apostles.* 1523–26. Panels, each 85 x 30″.
Pinakothek, Munich

LUCAS CRANACH THE ELDER. *Rest on the Flight to Egypt.* 1504. Panel, 27 x 20″.
Formerly State Museums, Berlin

Lucas Cranach the Elder. *The Judgment of Paris.* 1530. Panel,
13½ x 8¾". Staatliche Kunsthalle, Karlsruhe

ALBRECHT ALTDORFER. *Alexander the Great Defeating Darius (The Battle of Arbela).*
1529. Panel, 62 x 47″. Pinakothek, Munich

HANS HOLBEIN THE YOUNGER. *Erasmus of Rotterdam.* 1523. Panel, 16½ x 12½".
The Louvre, Paris. P: ARCH. PHOT.

· ANNO · ETATIS ·   SVÆ · XLIX ·

HANS HOLBEIN THE YOUNGER. *Henry VIII.* 1540. Panel, 32½ x 29″.
National Gallery, Rome. P: BROGI

JEAN CLOUET. *Francis I.* c. 1525–30. Panel, 37¾ x 29″.
The Louvre, Paris. P: GIRAUDON

MAERTEN VAN HEEMSKERK.
Family Portrait.
c. 1530. Panel,
46½ x 55″.
State Art Collections,
Kassel, Germany

PIETER AERTSEN.
A Meat Stall. 1551.
Panel, 48½ x 59".
Museum of Art,
Uppsala University,
Sweden

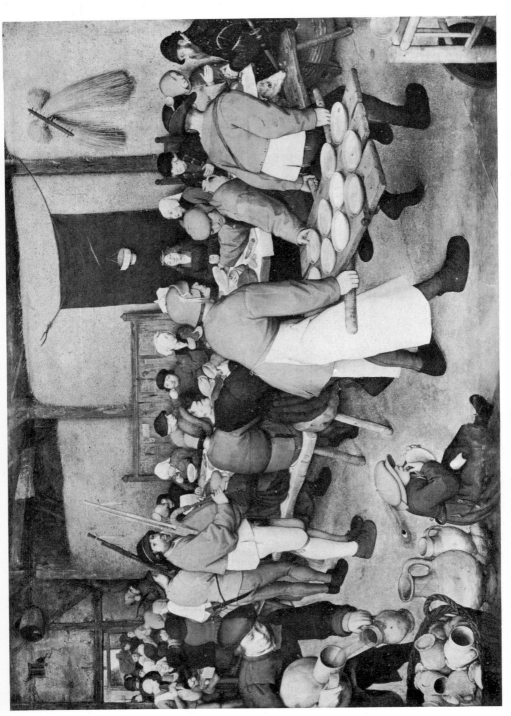

PIETER BRUEGEL THE ELDER. *Peasant Wedding.* c. 1565. Panel, 45 x 64″.
Kunsthistorisches Museum, Vienna

PIETER BRUEGEL THE ELDER. *The Blind Leading the Blind.* 1563.
34 x 66″. National Museum, Naples. P: ALINARI

EL GRECO. *Fray Felix Hortensio Paravicino.* c. 1605.
44½ x 33¾". Museum of Fine Arts, Boston

EL GRECO. *The Burial of Count Orgaz.* 1586. 16′ x 11′10″.
S. Tomé, Toledo, Spain. P: MAS

EL GRECO. *View of Toledo.* c. 1604–14. 47¾ x 42¾″. Metropolitan Museum of Art,
New York (Bequest of Mrs. H. O. Havemeyer, 1929. The H. O. Havemeyer Collection)

EL GRECO. *St. John's Vision of the Mysteries of the Apocalypse* (*The Opening of the Fifth Seal*). 1608-14. 88½ x 78¾". Metropolitan Museum of Art, New York (Rogers Fund, 1956)

LEFT

(A) JACQUES BELLANGE. *The Three Marys at the Tomb.* c. 1610. Etching. Metropolitan Museum of Art, (Dick Fund, 1930)

BELOW, LEFT

(B) JACQUES CALLOT. *Two Clowns,* from the series *Balli di Sfessania.* 1622. Etching. Metropolitan Museum of Art, (Dick Fund 1928)

BELOW, RIGHT

(C) JACQUES CALLOT. *A Beggar.* 1622. Etching. Metropolitan Museum of Art (Gift of Henry Walters, 1917)

Franca Trippa. *Fritellino.*

THE RENAISSANCE

21. *The Seventeenth Century in Italy*

GIANLORENZO BERNINI. *Model for Equestrian Statue of Louis XIV*. 1670. Terracotta, 30″. Borghese Gallery, Rome. P: GFN

(A) GIACOMO DELLA PORTA.
Façade, Church of the Gesù.
c. 1575–84. Rome. P: VINCENT

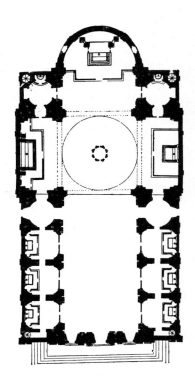

(B) GIACOMO VIGNOLA.
Plan of the Church of the Gesù.
1568. Rome

Andrea Sacchi and Jan Miel. *Urban VIII Visiting Il Gesù*.
1639–41. National Gallery, Rome. p: GFN

OPPOSITE PAGE
Interior,
Church of the Gesù.
Rome.

P: ANDERSON

RIGHT
G. B. GAULLI. *Triumph
of the Name of Jesus*
(ceiling fresco). 1672–85.
Church of the Gesù,
Rome.

P: KIDDER SMITH

Interior (with Bernini's Tabernacle, begun 1624),
St. Peter's. Rome. P: KIDDER SMITH

GIANLORENZO BERNINI. Throne of St. Peter. 1657–66. Gilt bronze, marble, and stucco.
Apse, St. Peter's, Rome. P: ANDERSON

OPPOSITE PAGE
Aerial view of St. Peter's,
Rome. (Nave and façade by
Carlo Maderna, 1606–26;
colonnade by Bernini,
begun 1656).

P: FOTOCIELO, ROME

RIGHT
FRANCESCO BORROMINI.
Façade, S. Agnese in
Piazza Navona. 1653–63.
Rome. P: ANDREWS

FRANCESCO BORROMINI. S. IVO. Begun 1642. Rome.

P: KIDDER SMITH

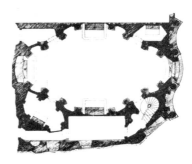

Francesco Borromini.
View and plan of S. Carlo alle Quattro Fontane.
Begun 1635 (façade 1667). Rome. p: anderson

Francesco Borromini.
Section and Interior of Dome, S. Ivo. Rome.

P: KIDDER SMITH

Francesco Borromini.
Interior views of S. Carlo alle Quattro Fontane, Rome.
P: ALINARI

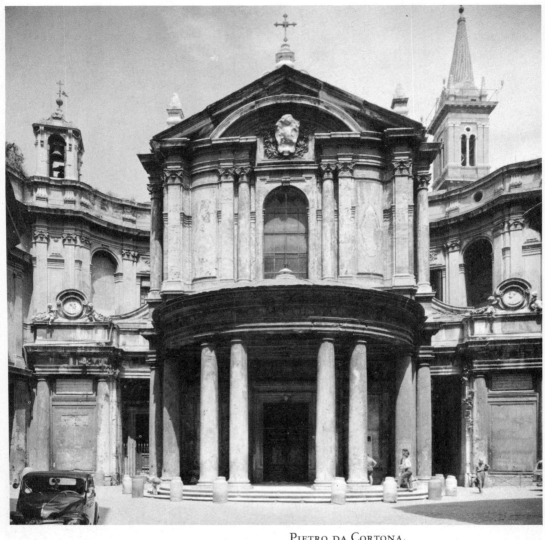

PIETRO DA CORTONA.
Façade and plan of S. Maria della Pace.
1656–57. Rome. P: VINCENT

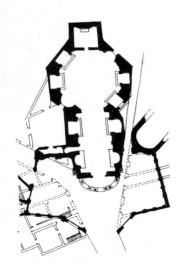

Baldassare Longhena.
View and plan of S. Maria della Salute.
Begun 1631. Venice. p: kidder smith

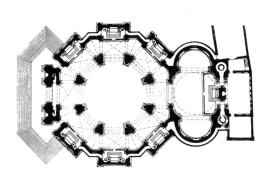

GUARINO GUARINI. Palazzo Carignano. Begun 1679. Turin.
P: KIDDER SMITH

GUARINO GUARINI.
Cappella della
Santissima Sindone
(Chapel of the
Holy Shroud).
1668–94.
Turin Cathedral.
P: KIDDER SMITH

GIANLORENZO BERNINI. *Bust of Costanza Buonarelli*. 1636–39. Marble, lifesize.
National Museum, Florence. P: ANDERSON

GIANLORENZO BERNINI. *David.* 1623. Marble, lifesize.
Borghese Gallery, Rome. P: GFN

GIANLORENZO BERNINI. *St. Longinus.* 1635–38. Marble, c. 14′6″.
St. Peter's, Rome. P: ALINARI

GIANLORENZO BERNINI. Tomb of Urban VIII. 1628–31, 1639–47. Bronze and marble. Apse, St. Peter's, Rome. P: A. RAICHLE, ULM

GIANLORENZO BERNINI. *The Ecstasy of St. Theresa.* 1645–52. Marble, lifesize.
Cornaro Chapel, S. Maria della Vittoria, Rome. P: ALINARI

CARAVAGGIO. *Bacchus*. c. 1590. 38½ x 33½". Uffizi Gallery,
Florence. P. SOPR. GALL. FLOR.

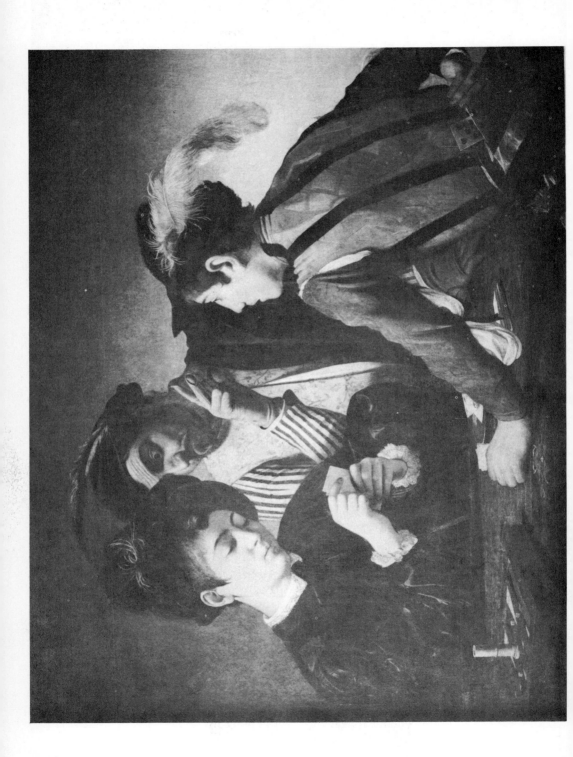

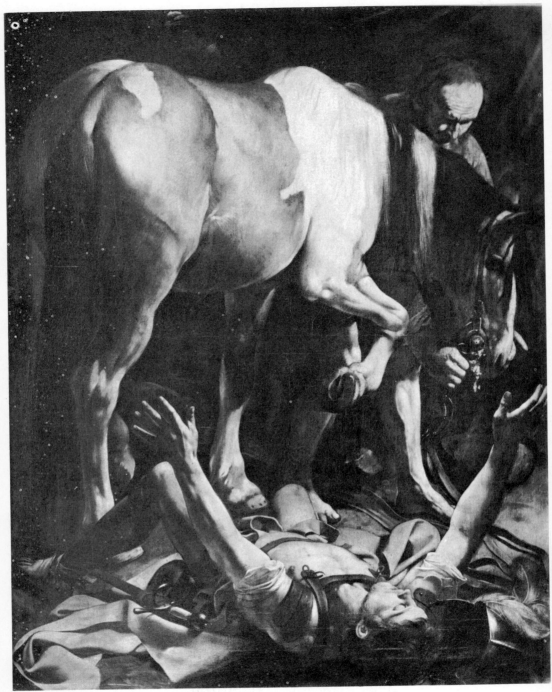

CARAVAGGIO. *Conversion of St. Paul.* 1601–2. 90½ x 69".
Cerasi Chapel, S. Maria del Popolo, Rome. P: ALINARI

ANNIBALE CARRACCI. Detail of ceiling fresco. 1597–1601.
Gallery, Palazzo Farnese, Rome. P: GFN

Annibale Carracci. *Landscape with the Flight into Egypt.* c. 1600. 48¼ x 90½".
Doria Gallery, Rome. p: ALINARI

Guido Reni. *Aurora* (ceiling fresco). c. 1614.
Casino Rospigliosi, Rome. p: Brogi

GUERCINO. *Aurora* (ceiling fresco). 1621–23.
Villa Ludovisi, Rome. P: ALINARI

THE RENAISSANCE

22. *The Seventeenth Century in Flanders, Holland, and Germany*

JAN VERMEER VAN DELFT. *View of Delft*. c. 1658.
38½ x 46¼". Mauritshuis, The Hague

Adam Elsheimer. *Landscape with the Temple of the Sibyl.* c. 1608.
Copper panel, 9½ x 13¾″. National Gallery, Prague

PETER PAUL RUBENS. *Drawing after Leonardo's Cartoon for "The Battle of Anghiari."*
c. 1605. The Louvre, Paris. P: GIRAUDON

PETER PAUL RUBENS. *Self-Portrait with Isabella Brant.* 1609–10. 69½ x 53½″.
Pinakothek, Munich

PETER PAUL RUBENS. *The Raising of the Cross.* 1610–11. Panel, 15′2″ x 11′2″.
Antwerp Cathedral. P: ACL

PETER PAUL RUBENS. *Marie de Medicis, Queen of France, Landing in Marseilles.*
1622–23. Oil sketch on panel, 25 x 19¾″. Pinakothek, Munich

PETER PAUL RUBENS. *Landscape with the Castle of Steen.* 1636.
Panel, 53 x 93". National Gallery, London

PETER PAUL RUBENS. *The Garden of Love.* c. 1632–34.
78 x 111½″. The Prado, Madrid. P: MAS

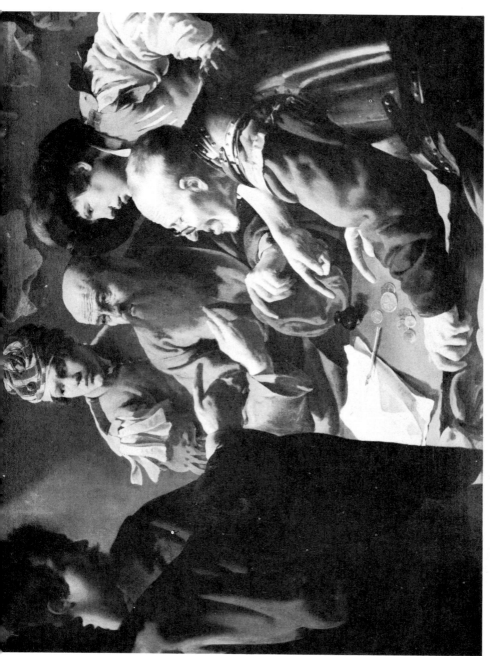

HENDRICK TERBRUGGHEN. *The Calling of St. Matthew.* 1621.
40 x 54". Centraal Museum, Utrecht

ANTHONY VAN DYCK. *Portrait of Charles I Hunting.* C. 1635. 107 x 83½".
The Louvre, Paris. P. ARCH. PHOT.

FRANS HALS. *The Laughing Cavalier.* 1624. 33 x 26¼".
Wallace Collection, London

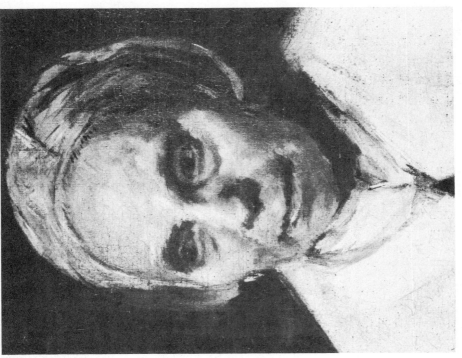

ABOVE

(B) Detail of p. 811

OPPOSITE PAGE

FRANS HALS. *The Women Regents of the Old Men's Home at Haarlem.*

(A) FRANS HALS. *Malle Babbe.* c. 1650.
29½ x 25″. Formerly State Museums, Berlin

LEFT

(A) REMBRANDT. *Tobit and Anna with the Kid.* 1626. Panel, 15½ x 11¾".
Collection Baroness Bentinck, Paris. P: RIJKSMUSEUM, AMSTERDAM

ABOVE

(B) REMBRANDT. *Study of a Man in a Turban* (portion).
c. 1637–40. Pen and wash drawing.

REMBRANDT.
*The Anatomy of
Dr. Tulp.*
1632. 66¾ x 85¼".
Mauritshuis,
The Hague

REMBRANDT.
The Blinding of Samson.
1636. 93 x 119".
Staedel Institute, Frankfurt

REMBRANDT. *The Night Watch*
(*The Company of Captain
Frans Banning Cocq*).
1642. 12′2″ x 14′7″.
Rijksmuseum, Amsterdam

REMBRANDT.
Christ Preaching.
c. 1652. Etching.
Metropolitan Museum
of Art, New York
(Bequest of
Mrs. H. O. Havemeyer,
1929)

REMBRANDT. *The Polish Rider.*
c. 1655. 46 x 53".
The Frick Collection,
New York

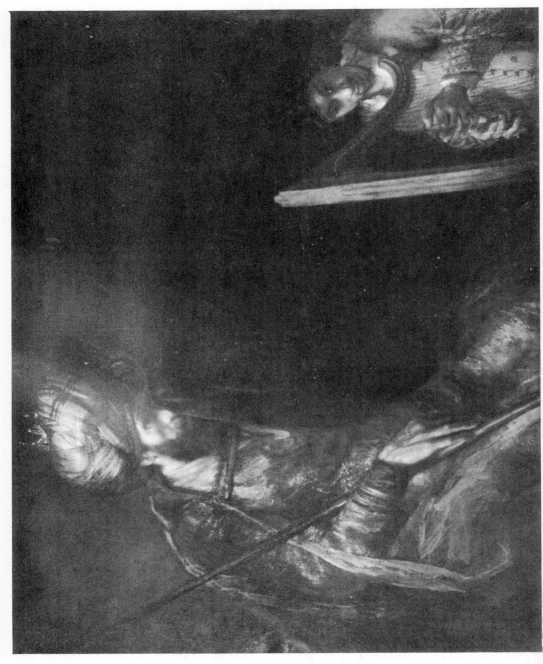

REMBRANDT. *Saul and David.*
c. 1660. 51½ x 64½".
Mauritshuis, The Hague

REMBRANDT.
Family Portrait.
c. 1668. 50 x 66½".
Municipal Museum,
Brunswick, Germany.
P: STADTBILDSTELLE,
BRUNSWICK

LEFT

(A) REMBRANDT. *Self-Portrait*. c. 1660. 45 x 38".
The Iveagh Bequest, Kenwood, London. P: © LONDON COUNTY COUNCIL

ABOVE

(B) REMBRANDT. *The Presentation in the Temple*. 1661. Pen and wash drawing. Royal Library, The Hague. P: A. FREQUIN, THE HAGUE

HERCULES SEGHERS. *Mountain Landscape.* c. 1630–35.
22 x 40″. Uffizi Gallery, Florence. P: BROGI

JACOB VAN RUISDAEL.
The Jewish Graveyard.
c. 1655. 32 x 37½".
State Picture Gallery,
Dresden.

P: F. BRUCKMANN, MUNICH

WILLEM CLAESZ. HEDA.
Still Life. 1634.
Panel, 17 x 22½".
Boymans Museum,
Rotterdam

(B) GERARD TERBORCH. *The Concert.* c. 1655–60. Panel,
22 x 17¼". Formerly State Museums, Berlin

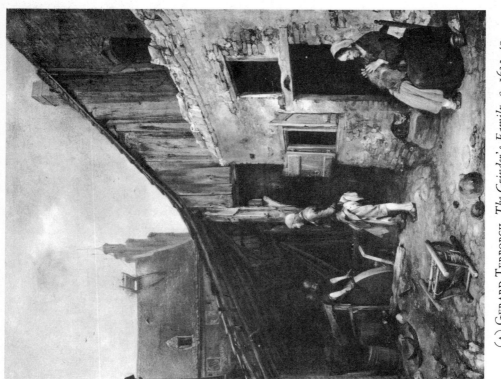

(A) GERARD TERBORCH. *The Grinder's Family.* c. 1635–40.
28½ x 23¼". Formerly State Museums, Berlin

JAN STEEN. *The Eve of St. Nicholas.* c. 1660–65.
32¼ x 27¾″. Rijksmuseum, Amsterdam

JAN VERMEER VAN DELFT. *The Girl with a Red Hat.* c. 1660. 9⅛ x 7⅛″.
National Gallery of Art, Washington, D. C. (Mellon Collection)

JAN VERMEER VAN DELFT. *The Artist in His Studio*. c. 1665–70.
52 x 44″. Kunsthistorisches Museum, Vienna

(A) PIETER SAENREDAM. *The St. Cunera Church, Rhenen.* 1655.
Panel, 19¾ x 27″. Mauritshuis, The Hague

(B) EMANUEL DE WITTE. *Interior of a Church.* 1668.
38¾ x 44″. Boymans Museum, Rotterdam

THE RENAISSANCE

23. The Seventeenth Century in France, England, and Spain

CLAUDE LORRAIN. *View of the Campagna.* c. 1650?
Wash drawing. British Museum, London

Claude Perrault. East Front of the Louvre. 1667–70. Paris. p: Andrews

Louis Le Vau and Jules Hardouin-Mansart. Garden Front, Palace of Versailles.
1669–85. P: VIZZAVONA

(A) Aerial view of the Palace of Versailles.
P: COMPAGNIE AÉRIENNE FRANÇAISE, SURESNES

(B) JULES HARDOUIN-MANSART and CHARLES LEBRUN. Galerie des Glâces. Begun 1678.
Palace of Versailles. P: JEAN-MARIE MARCEL, PARIS

Mansart, Lebrun, and Coysevox. Salon de la Guerre. Begun 1678.
Palace of Versailles. P: VIZZAVONA

JULES HARDOUIN-MANSART. Church of the Invalides.
1680–91. Paris. P: ROUBIER

(A) Inigo Jones. Banqueting House (west front). 1619–22. Whitehall Palace, London.

P: RCHM LONDON

(B) Sir Christopher Wren. South and East Fronts, Hampton Court Palace. Designed 1689. Middlesex. P: RCHM LONDON (CROWN COPYRIGHT)

SIR CHRISTOPHER WREN. Façade, St. Paul's Cathedral.
Begun 1675. London. P: NBR LONDON

SIR CHRISTOPHER WREN. Interior, St. Paul's Cathedral. London. P: EDWIN SMITH

PIERRE PUGET. *Herm*. 1656. Town Hall, Toulon.
P: ARCH. PHOT.

PIERRE PUGET. *Milo of Crotona.* 1671–83.
The Louvre, Paris. P: ALINARI

FRANÇOIS GIRARDON. Tomb of Richelieu (detail). 1675–77. Marble, figures lifesize.
Sorbonne Church, Paris. P: MARBURG

ANTOINE COYSEVOX. *Charles Lebrun.* 1676. Terracotta, 26″.
Wallace Collection, London

Diego Velázquez. *The Water Carrier of Seville*. c. 1619. 41½ x 31½".
Wellington Museum, London (Crown copyright reserved)

Diego Velázquez. *Infante Carlos*. c. 1625. 82 x 48".
The Prado, Madrid. P: MAS

DIEGO VELÁZQUEZ.
The Surrender of Breda.
1634–35. 10′1″ x 12′.
The Prado, Madrid. P: MAS

The Infanta Margarita-Maria
(detail of p. 846). P: ANDERSON

DIEGO VELÁZQUEZ. *The Maids of Honor.* 1656. 10′5″ x 9′.
The Prado, Madrid. P: ANDERSON

Francisco de Zurbarán. *St. Serapion.* 1628. 47½ x 40¾".
Wadsworth Atheneum, Hartford, Connecticut

RIGHT

SANCHEZ COTÁN.
Still Life.

c. 1602–5. 25 x 33½".
Museum, Granada.

P: STUDIOS PUYTORAC,
BORDEAUX

OPPOSITE PAGE

LOUIS LE NAIN.
Peasant Family.

c. 1640. 44½ x 62½".
The Louvre, Paris.

P: GIRAUDON

GEORGES DE LA TOUR. *Joseph the Carpenter.* C. 1645. 38½ x 25½".
The Louvre, Paris. P: BULLOZ

NICOLAS POUSSIN. *Self-Portrait*. 1650. 28¾ x 38½".
The Louvre, Paris. P: GIRAUDON

NICOLAS POUSSIN.
*The Rape of the
Sabine Women.*
c. 1636–37. 61 x 82½".
Metropolitan Museum
of Art, New York
(Dick Fund, 1946)

NICOLAS POUSSIN. *Landscape with the Burial of Phocion.* 1648. 70½ x 47".
The LOUVRE, PARIS. P: ARCH. PHOT.

THE RENAISSANCE

24. *The Eighteenth Century*

JOHANN KÄNDLER. *Two Freemasons Contemplating a Globe.* 1744.
Porcelain (Meissen ware), 9″. Collection Irwin Untermyer, New York

GERMAIN BOFFRAND.
Salon de la Princesse,
Hôtel de Soubise.
Begun 1732. Paris.

P: ANDREWS

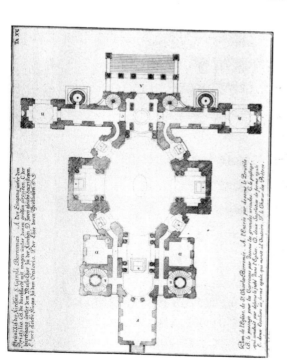

FISCHER VON ERLACH.
View and plan of St. Charles Borromaeus.
1716–37. Vienna.

P : SCHMIDT-GLASSNER

Lukas von Hildebrandt. Garden Front, Upper Belvedere. 1721–24.
Vienna. p: ANDREWS

LUKAS VON HILDEBRANDT. Entrance Hall and Staircase, Upper Belvedere.
Vienna. P: SCHMIDT-GLASSNER

Jakob Prandtauer.
The Monastery of Melk-on-the-Danube.
Begun 1702.
Austria. P: SCHMIDT-GLASSNER

PRANDTAUER, BEDUZZI,
and MUNGGENAST.
Interior,
Monastery Church.
Completed c. 1738.
Melk-on-the-Danube.

P: MARBURG

Cosmas and Egid Quirin Asam. High Altar, Monastery Church. 1718–25.
Rohr (near Regensburg), Bavaria. P: MARBURG

Dominikus Zimmermann.
Pilgrimage Church
"Die Wies."
1745–54.
Upper Bavaria.
P. HIRMER (ABOVE) AND
GEBR. METZ, TÜBINGEN

Matthäus Daniel Pöppelmann. The Zwinger. 1711–22. Dresden.

P: A. RENGER-PAATZSCH, WAMEL-DORF ÜBER SOEST I.W.

BALTHASAR NEUMANN. The Kaisersaal, Episcopal Palace. 1719–44.
Würzburg. P: DTSCH. KUNSTVERL.

IGNACIO VERGARA. Main Portal, Casa de Dos Aguas.
1740–44. Valencia. P: MARBURG

Sir John Vanbrugh. Blenheim Palace. Begun 1705. Oxfordshire.
P: EDWIN SMITH (ABOVE) AND © COUNTRY LIFE

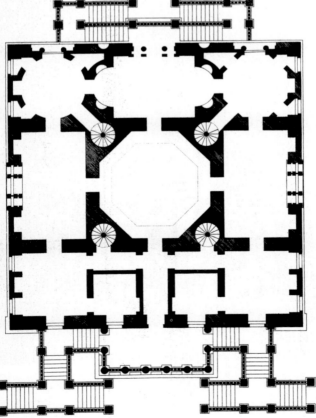

Lord Burlington.
View and plan of Chiswick House.
Begun 1725. Near London.
P: MINISTRY OF WORKS,
LONDON (CROWN COPYRIGHT)

JAMES GIBBS. St. Martin-in-the-Fields. 1721–26.
London. P: RAYMOND R. BUCKLEY, BOSTON

Andreas Schlüter. *Equestrian Monument of the Great Elector.* 1698–1703.
Bronze, over lifesize. Berlin-Charlottenburg. p: schmidt-glassner

ETIENNE MAURICE FALCONET. *Equestrian Monument of Peter the Great.* 1766–82.
Bronze, over lifesize. Leningrad. P: MARTIN HÜRLIMANN, from
Moscow and Leningrad, LONDON, THAMES & HUDSON, 1958

Jean-Baptiste Pigalle. *Tomb of the Maréchal de Saxe*. 1753–76.
Marble, statues approximately lifesize. St. Thomas', Strasbourg. P: BULLOZ

OPPOSITE PAGE

Giacomo Serpotta. *Fortitude*. 1714–17. Stucco. Oratorio della Compagnia
del Rosario, S. Domenico, Palermo. P: ALINARI

CLODION. *Satyr and Bacchante.* c. 1775. Terracotta, 23".
Metropolitan Museum of Art, New York (Bequest of Benjamin Altman, 1913)

Jean Antoine Houdon. *Voltaire.* 1781. Terracotta model for marble, 47″.
Fabre Museum, Montpellier, France. p: GIRAUDON

JEAN ANTOINE HOUDON. *George Washington.* 1788–92. Marble, 74″.
State Capitol, Richmond, Virginia. P: WHITAKER STUDIOS, RICHMOND

ANTOINE WATTEAU. *Gilles.* c. 1719. 73 x 59".
The Louvre, Paris. P: ARCH. PHOT.

Jean Honoré Fragonard.
Bathers. c. 1765.
25¼ x 31½".
The Louvre, Paris.

Jean-Baptiste Greuze.
The Village Bride.
1761. 36 x 46½".
The Louvre, Paris.

P: ARCH. PHOT.

JEAN ETIENNE LIOTARD. *Mary Gunning, Countess of Coventry, in Turkish Costume.*
c. 1754. Pastel, 39½ x 29½″. Rijksmuseum, Amsterdam

JEAN-BAPTISTE SIMÉON CHARDIN. *Back from the Market.* 1739. 18 x 14½″.
The Louvre, Paris. P: GIRAUDON

Jean-Baptiste Siméon Chardin.
Kitchen Still Life.
c. 1730–35. 12½ x 15¼".
Ashmolean Museum, Oxford

Francesco Guardi.
*View of an Island in
the Lagoon.* c. 1790.
14¼ x 19¼".
Collection Borletti,
Milan.

P: FIORENTINI

GIOVANNI BATTISTA TIEPOLO. *The Banquet of Cleopatra*. 1757.
Palazzo Labia, Venice. P: ANDERSON

GIOVANNI BATTISTA TIEPOLO. Detail of the ceiling fresco of the Kaisersaal
(see p. 865). 1751. Episcopal Palace, Würzburg.

P: CARL LAMB, FROM M. V. FREEDEN AND C. LAMB, *Tiepolo*, HIRMER VERLAG, MUNICH

WILLIAM HOGARTH. *The Orgy*,
scene III from
The Rake's Progress. c. 1734.
24½ x 29½".
Sir John Soane's Museum,
London

THOMAS GAINSBOROUGH. *Robert Andrews and His Wife.* c. 1748–50. 27 x 47″.
Collection G. W. Andrews, Redhill, Surrey, England. P: VIZZAVONA

WILLIAM HOGARTH. *The Graham Children*. 1742. 63 x 71″.
Tate Gallery, London

Thomas Gainsborough. *Mrs. Siddons.* 1785. 49½ x 39".
National Gallery, London

SIR JOSHUA REYNOLDS. *Mrs. Siddons as the Tragic Muse.* 1784. 93 x 57½″.
Henry E. Huntington Library and Art Gallery, San Marino, California

PART FIVE

THE MODERN WORLD

LIST OF ILLUSTRATIONS

25. CLASSICISM AND ROMANTICISM

26. REALISM AND IMPRESSIONISM

THE MODERN WORLD

25. *Classicism and Romanticism*

GEORGE CALEB BINGHAM. *Fur Traders on the Missouri.* c. 1845. 29 x 36".
Metropolitan Museum of Art, New York (Morris K. Jesup Fund, 1933)

(A) PETER HARRISON.
The Brick Market.
1761–62. Newport,
Rhode Island.
P: ANDREWS

(B) THOMAS JEFFERSON. Monticello. 1796–1806.
Charlottesville, Virginia. P: ANDREWS

Horace Walpole, with William Robinson and Others. Strawberry Hill. 1749–77. Twickenham, England. p: kersting (above) and © *Country Life*, london

RIGHT
JOHN NASH.
The Royal Pavilion.
1815–18.
Brighton, England.
P: EDWIN SMITH

OPPOSITE PAGE
SIR CHARLES BARRY
and A. W. N. PUGIN.
The Houses of
Parliament.
Begun 1835. London.
P: NBR LONDON

BENJAMIN LATROBE. Baltimore Cathedral. Begun 1805. Maryland.

P: J. H. SCHAEFER, BALTIMORE

RICHARD UPJOHN.
Trinity Church.
Completed 1846.
New York.
P: ANDREWS

CHARLES GARNIER. Grand Staircase, L'Opéra. 1861–74.
Paris. P: GIRAUDON

(A) Façade, L'Opéra. Paris. P: GIRAUDON

(B) HENRI LABROUSTE. Reading Room, Bibliothèque
Ste. Geneviève. 1843–50. Paris. P: MARBURG

ANTONIO CANOVA. *Pauline Borghese as Venus.* 1808. Marble, lifesize.
Borghese Gallery, Rome. P: ANDERSON

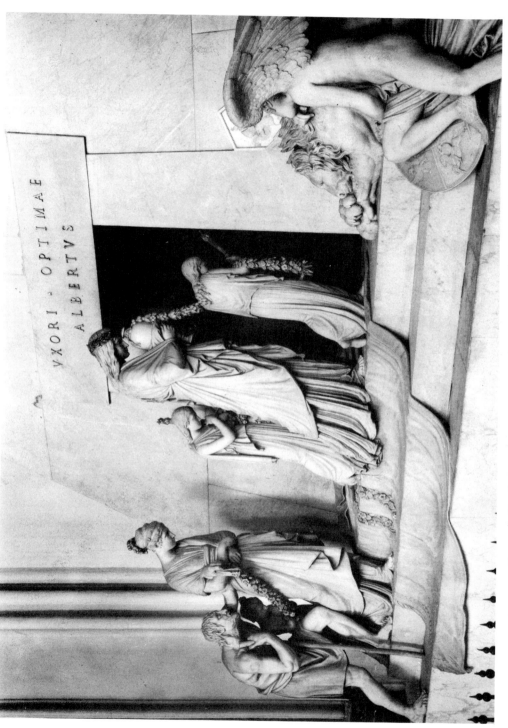

VXORI · OPTIMAE
ALBERTVS

Antonio Canova. *Tomb of the Countess Maria Christina.* 1798–1805. Marble statues, lifesize.
Church of the Augustinians, Vienna. P: EVA KRAFT, BUNDESDENKMALAMT, VIENNA

FRANÇOIS RUDE. *La Marseillaise (Departure of the Volunteers of 1792)*. 1833–36. c. 42 x 26′. Arc de Triomphe, Paris. P: BULLOZ

ABOVE

(A) JEAN FRANÇOIS CHALGRIN.
Arc de Triomphe. Begun 1806.
Paris. P: GIRAUDON

RIGHT

(B) FRANÇOIS RUDE.
Monument to Marshal Ney.
1853. Bronze, 8′9″.
Paris.
P: PIERRE DEVINOY,
PARIS

JEAN-BAPTISTE CARPEAUX. *The Dance*. 1867–69. c. 15′ x 8′6″.
Façade, L'Opéra. Paris. P: ROUBIER

(A) ANTOINE-LOUIS BARYE. *Jaguar Devouring a Hare.* 1850–51. Bronze, 16½ x 37½".
The Louvre, Paris. P: ALINARI

(B) JOSEPH WRIGHT OF DERBY. *An Experiment with the Air Pump.* 1768.
72 x 96". Tate Gallery, London

Benjamin West.
*The Death of
General Wolfe.*
1770. 59½ x 84″.
National Gallery
of Canada,
Ottawa

JOHN SINGLETON COPLEY.
Watson and the Shark.
1778. 72½ x 90¼″.
Museum of Fine Arts,
Boston

JOHN SINGLETON COPLEY. *Mrs. Thomas Boylston.* 1766. 50½ x 40½".
Fogg Art Museum, Harvard University, Cambridge, Massachusetts

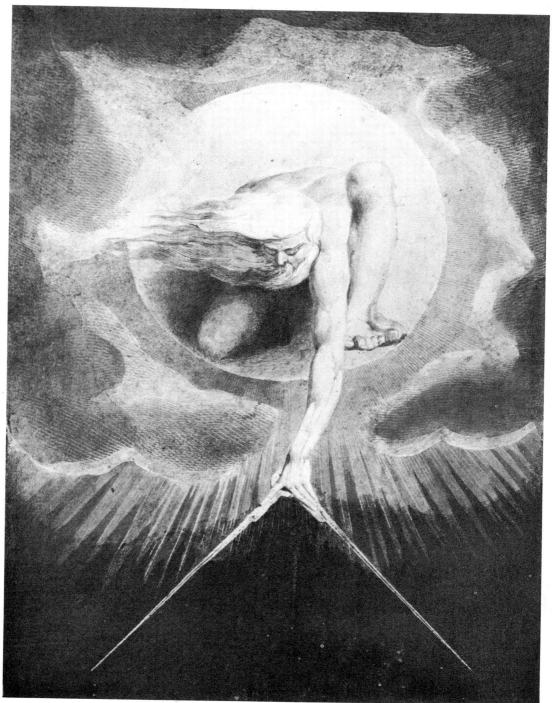

WILLIAM BLAKE. *The Ancient of Days*, frontispiece of *Europe, a Prophecy*. 1794.
Metal relief etching, hand-colored. Library of Congress, Washington, D. C.
(Lessing J. Rosenwald Collection)

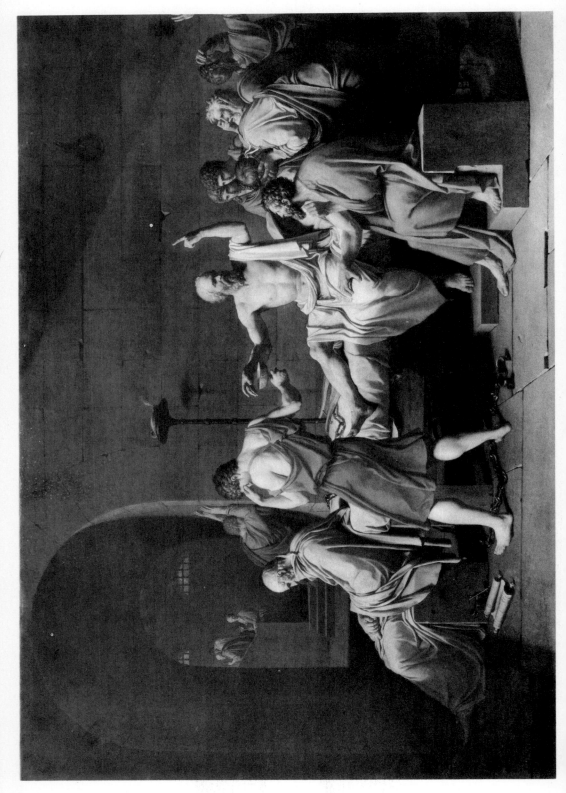

Jacques Louis David. *The Death of Marat.* 1793. 65 x 50½″.
Royal Museums of Fine Arts, Brussels. P: ACL

ANTOINE-JEAN GROS. *Napoleon at the Bridge of Arcole.* 1796. 29½ x 23".
The Louvre, Paris. P: GIRAUDON

Jacques Louis David.
Madame Julie Récamier.
1800. 68 x 96".
The Louvre, Paris.
P: ARCH. PHOT.

J. A. D. INGRES. *Odalisque.* 1814. 36 x 64″.
The Louvre, Paris. P: ALINARI

J. A. D. INGRES. *Louis Bertin*. 1832. Pencil drawing.
The Louvre, Paris. P: BULLOZ

J. A. D. INGRES. *Louis Bertin.* 1832. 46 x 37½".
The Louvre, Paris. P: GIRAUDON

Francisco Goya.
The Family of Charles IV.
1800. 9′ 2″ x 11′.
The Prado, Madrid.

P: MAS

Francisco Goya.
The Third of May, 1808.
1814–15. 8' 9" x 13' 4".
The Prado, Madrid.

P: MAS

Francisco Goya.
Bobabilicon
(*Big Booby*), No. 4 of
the series of etchings
Los Proverbios. c. 1818.
Metropolitan Museum
of Art, New York
(Dick Fund, 1931)

ALEXANDER COZENS.
Landscape Made of Ink Blots,
aquatint from
*A New Method of
Assisting the Invention
in Drawing Original
Compositions of Landscape.*
1784–86.
Metropolitan Museum
of Art, New York
(Rogers Fund, 1906)

John Constable.
Weymouth Bay.
1816. 21 x 29¼″.
National Gallery,
London

JOHN CONSTABLE.
Stoke-by-Nayland.
1836. 49½ x 66½".
The Art Institute
of Chicago

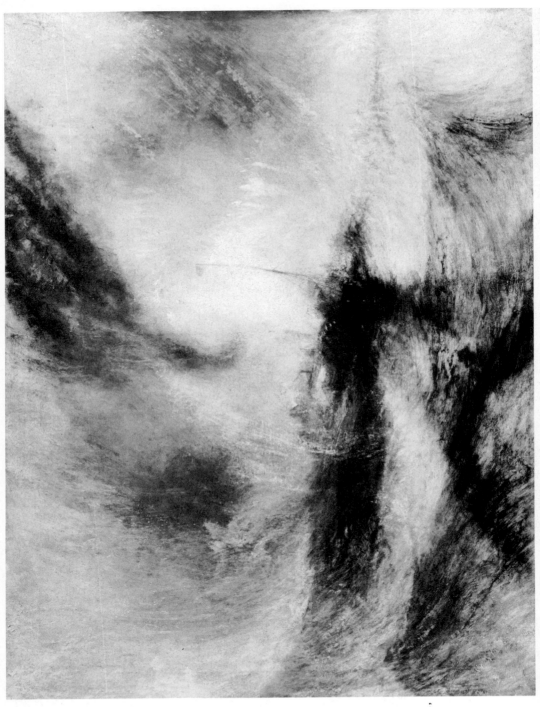

THÉODORE GÉRICAULT. *Mounted Officer of the Imperial Guard*. 1812.
9′7″ x 6′4½″. The Louvre, Paris. P: ARCH. PHOT.

EUGÈNE DELACROIX. *The Massacre of Chios*. 1824. 13′10″ x 11′7″.
The Louvre, Paris. P: VIZZAVONA

THÉODORE GÉRICAULT. *The Madman*. 1821–24. 24 x 20".
Museum of Fine Arts, Ghent. P: BULLOZ

Eugène Delacroix. *Frédéric Chopin.* 1838. 18 x 15″.
The Louvre, Paris. P: GIRAUDON

Eugène Delacroix. *The Abduction of Rebecca.* 1846. 39½ x 32¼".
Metropolitan Museum of Art, New York (Wolfe Fund, 1903)

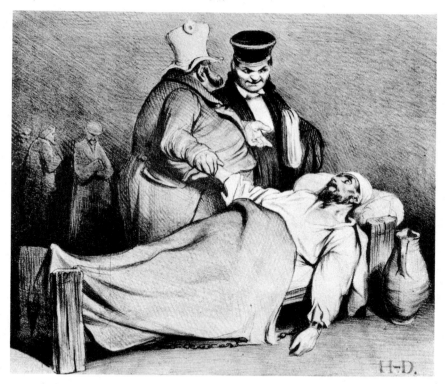

(A) HONORÉ DAUMIER. *It's Safe to Release This One!*
1834. Lithograph. Metropolitan Museum of Art,
New York (Dick Fund, 1941)

(B) HONORÉ DAUMIER. *The Soup.* c. 1860–70. Pen and wash drawing.
The Louvre, Paris. P: GIRAUDON

Caspar David Friedrich.
*The Wreck of the
"Hoffnung."* 1821.
38½ x 50½".
Kunsthalle, Hamburg

CAMILLE COROT.
*View of Tivoli from
the Villa d'Este.*
1843. 17 x 23½".
Collection Mr. and
Mrs. René Lecomte,
Paris.

P: VIZZAVONA

CAMILLE COROT. *The Interrupted Reading.* c. 1865–70. 36 x 25½".
The Art Institute of Chicago (Potter Palmer Collection)

THE MODERN WORLD

26. *Realism and Impressionism*

JAMES WHISTLER. *Arrangement in Black and Gray (The Artist's Mother)*. 1871. 57 x 64½".
The Louvre, Paris. P: VIZZAVONA

GUSTAVE COURBET. *The Stone Breakers.* 1849. 63 x 102". Formerly State Picture Gallery, Dresden (destroyed ?). P: F. BRUCKMANN, MUNICH

GUSTAVE COURBET. *The Painter's Studio* (*Une allégorie réelle*).
1854–55. The Louvre, Paris. P: GIRAUDON

ABOVE
FRANÇOIS MILLET. *The Sower.* c. 1850. 40 x 32½".
Museum of Fine Arts, Boston

OPPOSITE PAGE
EDOUARD MANET. *The Fifer.* 1866. 63 x 38".
The Louvre, Paris

Edouard Manet.
Luncheon on the Grass
(Le déjeuner sur l'herbe).
1863. 84 x 106".
The Louvre, Paris.
P: ARCH. PHOT.

EDOUARD MANET.
*A Bar at the
Folies-Bergère.*
1881–82. 37½ x 51".
The Courtauld
Collection,
Home House, London.
P: © *Country Life,*
LONDON

CLAUDE MONET. *The River.*
1868. 32 x 39½".
The Art Institute of Chicago
(Potter Palmer Collection)

AUGUSTE RENOIR.
Le Moulin de la Galette.
1876. 51½ x 69″.
The Louvre, Paris.
P: BULLOZ

AUGUSTE RENOIR. *Study for "The Bathers."* c. 1885. 49½ x 43½".
Fogg Art Museum, Harvard University, Cambridge, Massachusetts (Wertheim Collection)

EDGAR DEGAS. *Edouard Manet*. c. 1865. Pencil drawing.
Metropolitan Museum of Art, New York (Rogers Fund, 1918)

EDGAR DEGAS. *Prima Ballerina*. C. 1876. Pastel, 23 x 16½".
The Louvre, Paris. P: ARCH. PHOT.

EDGAR DEGAS. *The Glass of Absinthe.* 1876. 36 x 27″.
The Louvre, Paris. P: GIRAUDON

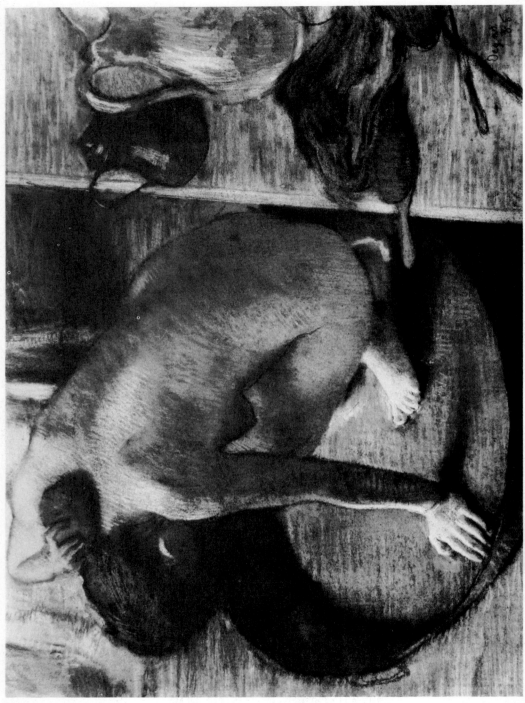

RIGHT

EDGAR DEGAS.
The Tub.
1886. Pastel,
23½ x 32½".
The Louvre, Paris.
P: ARCH. PHOT.

OPPOSITE PAGE

WINSLOW HOMER.
The Morning Bell.
c. 1866. 24 x 38".
Collection Stephen
C. Clark, New York

THOMAS EAKINS. *The Gross Clinic*. 1875. 96 x 78".
Jefferson Medical College, Philadelphia. P: PHILADELPHIA MUSEUM OF ART

AUGUSTE RODIN. *Jules Dalou*. 1883. Bronze, lifesize.
The Louvre, Paris. P: GIRAUDON

AUGUSTE RODIN. *The Thinker*. 1889. Bronze, 27½".
Metropolitan Museum of Art, New York (Gift of Thomas F. Ryan, 1910)

Auguste Rodin. *The Kiss*. 1896. Marble, lifesize.
Rodin Museum, Paris. P: ALINARI

Auguste Rodin. *Balzac* (portion). 1892–97. Plaster, 9′10″.
Rodin Museum, Paris. P: VIZZAVONA

Constantin Meunier. *Longshoreman*. 1893. Bronze, c. 86″.
The Louvre, Paris. p: ALINARI

EDGAR DEGAS.
*Dancer Looking
at the Sole of Her
Right Foot.* 1882–95.
Bronze, 18″.
P: LEONARD VON MATT,
COURTESY CONZETT &
HUBER, ZURICH

THE MODERN WORLD

27. *Post-Impressionism and "Art Nouveau"*

ARISTIDE MAILLOL. *Seated Woman (Méditerranée).* c. 1901. 41″.
Collection Dr. Oskar Reinhart, Winterthur, Switzerland

Louis Sullivan. Wainright Building. 1890–91. St. Louis, Missouri.

P: RICHARD NICKEL, PARK RIDGE, ILL.

OPPOSITE PAGE, ABOVE AND BELOW

Louis Sullivan. Carson Pirie Scott Store. 1899. Chicago.

P: RICHARD NICKEL, PARK RIDGE, ILL.

Henry van de Velde. Werkbund Theater. 1914. Cologne.

P: COURTESY RIJKSMUSEUM KRÖLLER-MÜLLER, OTTERLO, HOLLAND

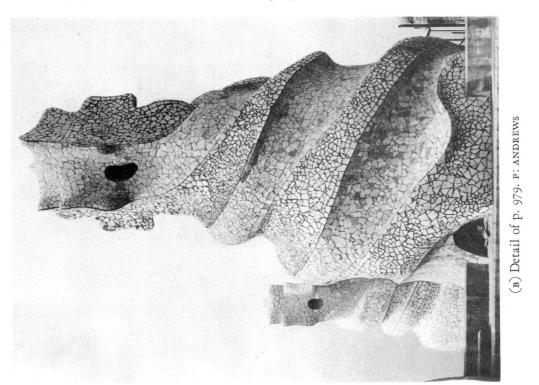

(B) Detail of p. 979. P: ANDREWS

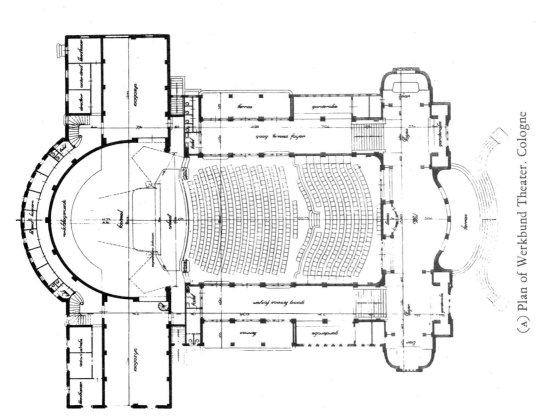

(A) Plan of Werkbund Theater. Cologne

(A) Paul Cézanne, after Sebastiano del Piombo.
Christ in Limbo. c. 1868–70. 66 x 40″.
Collection Mr. and Mrs. René Lecomte, Paris.
P: BULLOZ

RIGHT

(B) Sebastiano del Piombo. *Christ in Limbo*.
c. 1530. 89 x 45″. The Prado, Madrid.
P: MAS

PAUL CÉZANNE. *Self-Portrait*. 1879–82. 25½ x 20″.
Museum of Art, Bern, Switzerland

PAUL CÉZANNE.
Fruit Bowl, Glass, and Apples.
1879–82. 18 x 21½″.
Collection Mr. and Mrs. René
Lecomte, Paris.
P: VIZZAVONA

PAUL CÉZANNE.
*Mont Sainte-Victoire
Seen from Bibemus Quarry.*
c. 1898–1900. 25½ x 32".
Baltimore Museum of Art
(The Cone Collection)

OPPOSITE PAGE

GEORGES SEURAT.
Sideshow (La parade).
1889. 39½ x 59½".
Collection Stephen
C. Clark, New York.
P: MUSEUM OF MODERN
ART, NEW YORK

RIGHT

VINCENT VAN GOGH.
The Potato Eaters.
1885. 32¼ x 45".
Collection V. W. van
Gogh, Laren, Holland

VINCENT VAN GOGH. *Self-Portrait*. 1889. 22½ x 17″. Collection Ambassador and Mrs. John Hay Whitney, New York. P: M. KNOEDLER & CO., INC., NEW YORK

PAUL GAUGUIN. *The Yellow Christ.* 1889. 36½ x 29".
Albright Art Gallery, Buffalo, New York

VINCENT VAN GOGH.
Starry Night.
1889. Pen drawing.
Formerly Kunsthalle,
Bremen (destroyed ?)

PAUL GAUGUIN.
The Day of the God.
1894. 26 x 34¼".
The Art Institute of
Chicago (Helen
Birch Bartlett
Memorial Collection)

HENRI ROUSSEAU. *The Sleeping Gypsy.* 1897. 51 x 70".
Museum of Modern Art, New York (Gift of Mrs. Simon Guggenheim)

JAMES ENSOR. *Intrigue*. 1890. 35½ x 59″.
Royal Museum of Fine Arts, Antwerp. P: ACL

EDVARD MUNCH. *The Scream.* 1893. 36 x 29″. National Gallery, Oslo

PABLO PICASSO. *The Old Guitarist*. 1903. 47¾ x 32½".
The Art Institute of Chicago (Helen Birch Bartlett Memorial Collection)

CLAUDE MONET. *Water-Lilies, Giverny.* 1907. 36½ x 29".
Collection Jocelyn Walker, London. P: THE ARTS COUNCIL OF GREAT BRITAIN

THE MODERN WORLD

28. The Twentieth Century

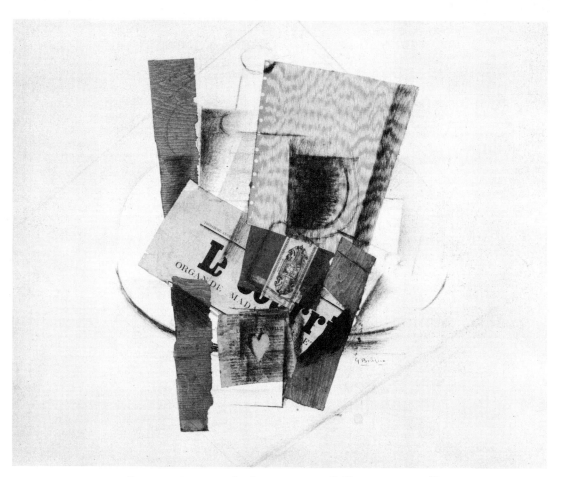

(B) Auguste Perret. Notre Dame du Raincy. 1922–23. Paris. P: Kidder Smith

ABOVE

(A) Walter Gropius. Plan of the Bauhaus. 1925–26. Dessau, Germany

Machine Shop, The Bauhaus, Dessau. P: MUSEUM OF MODERN ART, NEW YORK

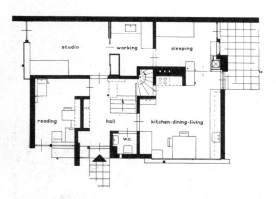

GERRIT RIETVELD. View and plans,
Schröder House. 1924. Utrecht.
(Plans after Theodore M. Brown.)
P: JAN VERSNEL, AMSTERDAM

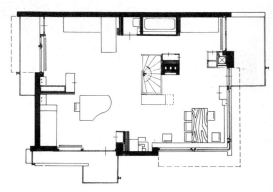

Le Corbusier. Savoye House. 1929–30. Poissy-sur-Seine.
P: LUCIEN HERVÉ, PARIS

Howe and Lescaze. Philadelphia Savings Fund Society Building. 1931–32. Philadelphia. P: COURTESY WILLIAM LESCAZE, NEW YORK

MIES VAN DER ROHE. Lake Shore Drive Apartments. 1950–52. Chicago.
P: HEDRICH-BLESSING, CHICAGO

Le Corbusier. Unité d'Habitation Apartment House. 1947–52. Marseilles.   P: KIDDER SMITH

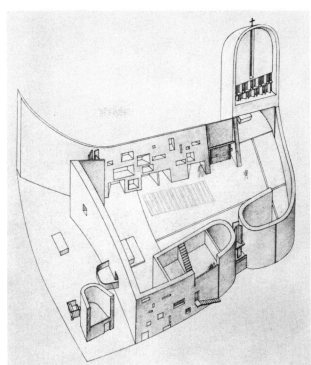

RIGHT AND BELOW
LE CORBUSIER. Notre Dame du Haut.
1950–55. Ronchamp.
P: LUCIEN HERVÉ, PARIS

Interior, Notre Dame du Haut. Ronchamp.

P: LUCIEN HERVÉ, PARIS

ERNST BARLACH. *Man Drawing a Sword.* 1911. Wood, 31″. Museum, Cranbrook Academy of Art, Bloomfield Hills, Michigan. P: ADOLPH STUDLY, NEW YORK

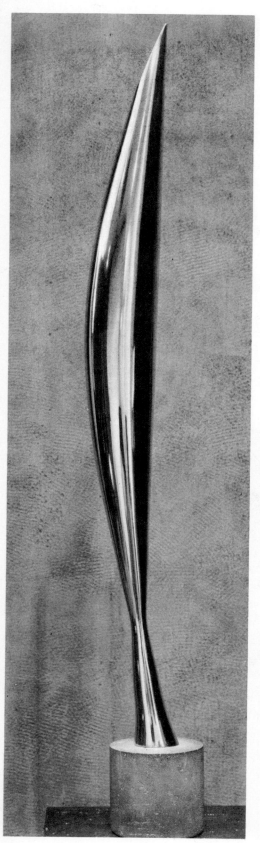

Umberto Boccioni. *Unique Forms of Continuity in Space.* 1913. Bronze, 43½″.
Museum of Modern Art, New York (Acquired through the Lillie P. Bliss Bequest)

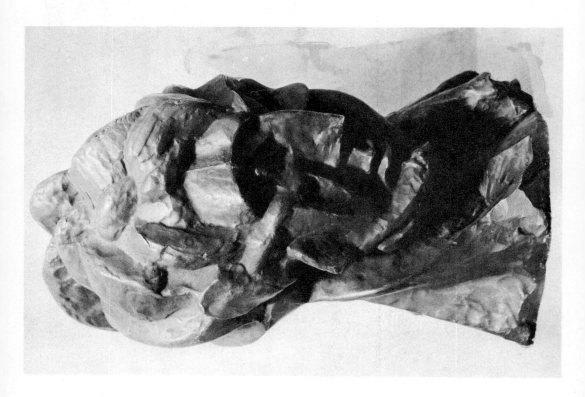

PABLO PICASSO. *The She-Goat*. 1950. Bronze (cast in May 1952), 46⅜ x 56⅜".
Museum of Modern Art, New York (Mrs. Simon Guggenheim Fund)

(A) ALBERTO GIACOMETTI. *Woman with Her Throat Cut*. 1932. Bronze, 34½" long.
Museum of Modern Art, New York (Purchase)

(B) JULIO GONZALEZ. *Head*. 1935? Wrought iron, 17¾".
Museum of Modern Art, New York (Purchase)

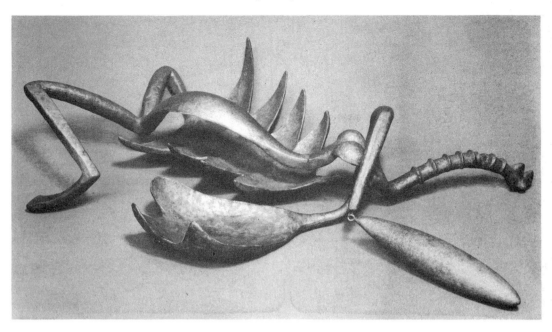

HANS ARP. *Egg Board.* 1922. Painted wood, 29½ x 39".
Collection Graindorge, Liège. P: OLIVER BAKER, NEW YORK

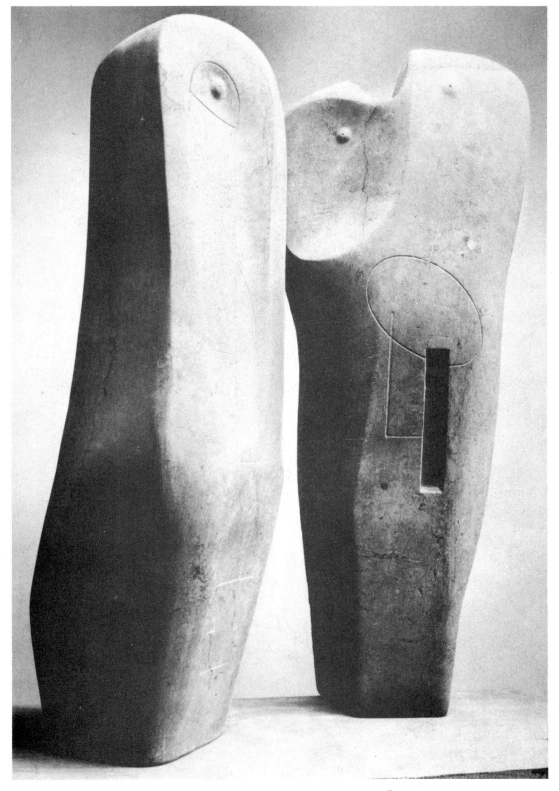

HENRY MOORE. *Two Forms*. 1936. C. 42″.
Collection the late Sir Michael Sadleir. P: COURTESY HENRY MOORE

Henry Moore. *Recumbent Figure.* 1938. c. 54" long. Tate Gallery, London. p: Henry Moore

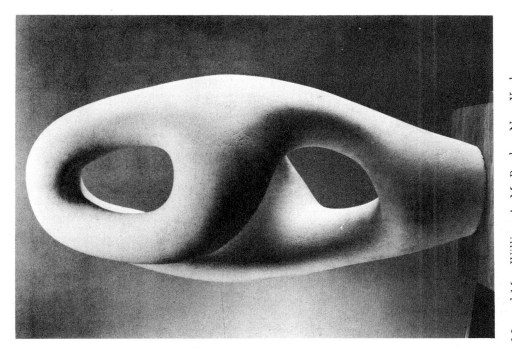

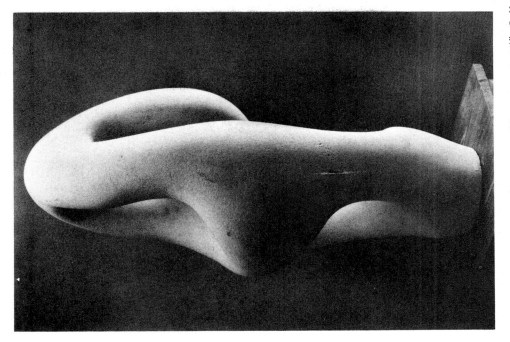

Hans Arp. *Ptolemy*. 1953. Limestone, 40½″. Collection Mr. and Mrs. William A. M. Burden, New York.

P: ADOLPH STUDLY, NEW YORK

ALEXANDER CALDER. *Lobster Trap and Fish Tail* (mobile). 1939.
Steel wire and sheet aluminum, c. 8′6″ x 9′6″.
Museum of Modern Art, New York (Gift of the Advisory Committee)

HENRY MOORE. *The Bride*. 1940. Lead and copper wire, 9⅜″.
Museum of Modern Art, New York (Acquired through the Lillie P. Bliss Bequest)

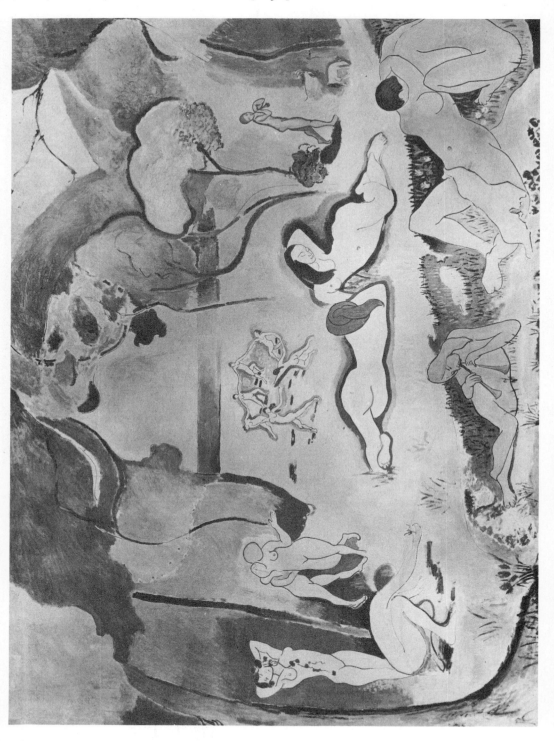

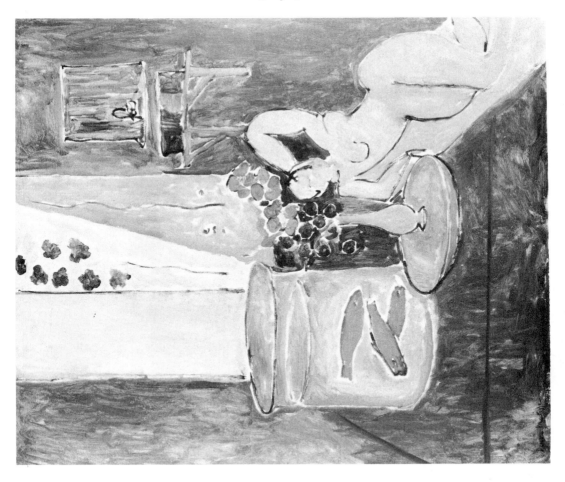

GEORGES ROUAULT. *Head of Christ*. 1905. Paper on canvas, 45 x 31".
Collection Walter P. Chrysler, Jr., New York. P: BARNEY BURSTEIN, BOSTON

GEORGES ROUAULT. *The Old Clown.* 1917. 44¼ x 29½".
Collection Stavros Niarchos. P: MUSEUM OF MODERN ART, NEW YORK

WASSILY KANDINSKY. *Improvisation No. 30.* 1913.
43¼" square. The Art Institute of Chicago
(Arthur Jerome Eddy Memorial Collection)

EMIL NOLDE
The Last Supper.
1909. 32½ x 41¾".
Stiftung Seebüll
Ada und Emil Nolde,
Neukirchen (Schleswig),
Germany.

P: KLEINHEMPEL, HAMBURG

CHAIM SOUTINE. *Dead Fowl*. c. 1926. 38½ x 24½".
The Art Institute of Chicago (Joseph Winterbotham Collection)

(B) MAX BECKMANN. *The Dream*.
1921. 71 x 35".
Collection Benno Elkan, London

(A) OSKAR KOKOSCHKA. *Self-Portrait*.
1913. 32⅛ x 19½".
Museum of Modern Art,
New York (Purchase)

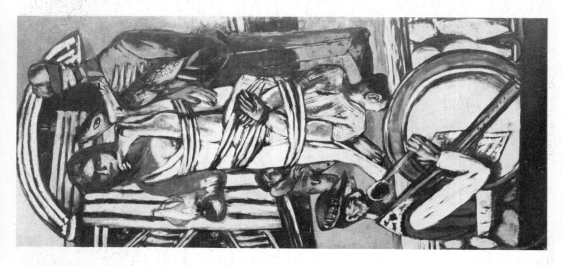

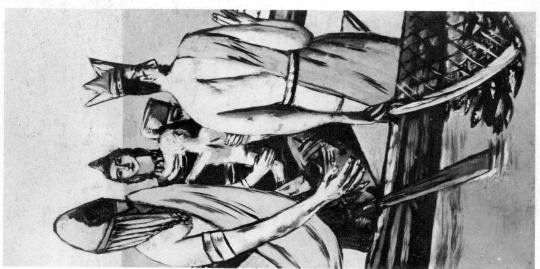

OPPOSITE PAGE

MAX BECKMANN.
Departure (triptych). 1932–35.
center panel 84¾ x 45⅜″,
side panels each 84¾ x 39¼″.
Museum of Modern Art, New York

RIGHT

JOSÉ CLEMENTE OROZCO.
Modern Migration of the Spirit. 1932–34. Fresco.
Baker Library, Dartmouth College,
Hanover, New Hampshire

PABLO PICASSO. *Les demoiselles d'Avignon.* 1907. 96 x 92".
Museum of Modern Art, New York (Acquired through the Lillie P. Bliss Bequest)

PABLO PICASSO. *Ambroise Vollard.* 1909–10. 36 x 25½″.
Pushkin Museum, Moscow. P: BIJTEBIER

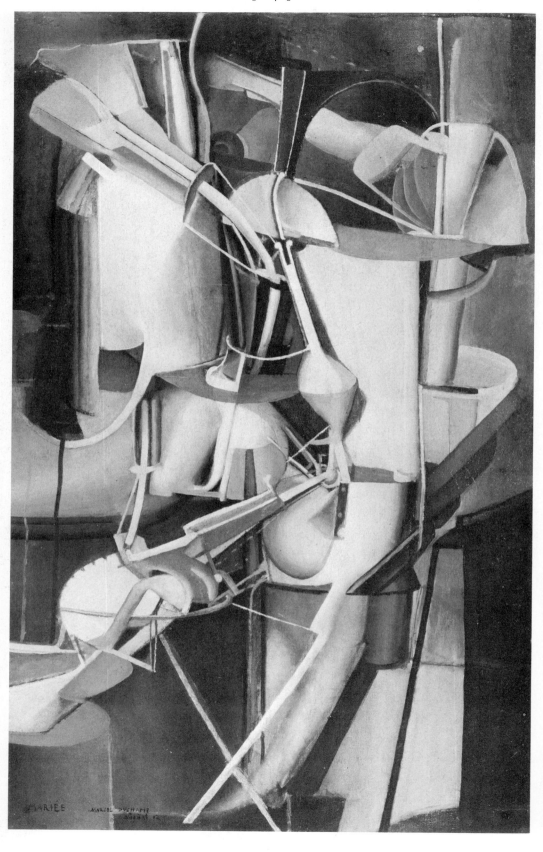

ABOVE

JOSEPH STELLA. *Brooklyn Bridge*. 1917. 84 x 76″. Yale University Art Gallery,
New Haven, Connecticut (Collection of the Société Anonyme)

OPPOSITE PAGE

MARCEL DUCHAMP. *The Bride*. 1912. 34¾ x 21½″.
Philadelphia Museum of Art (Louise and Walter Arensberg Collection)

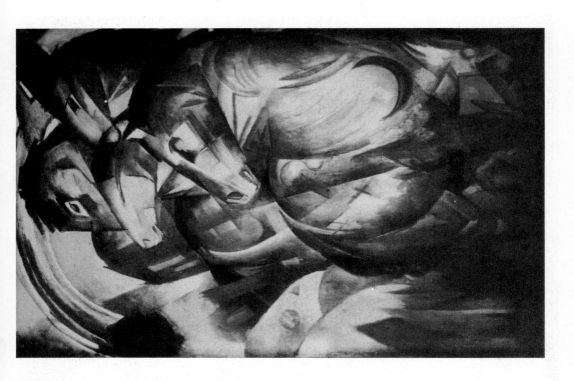

OPPOSITE PAGE

PIET MONDRIAN.
Flowering Trees. 1912.
25½ x 29½". Collection
G. J. Nieuwenhuizen
Segaar Art Gallery, The Hague

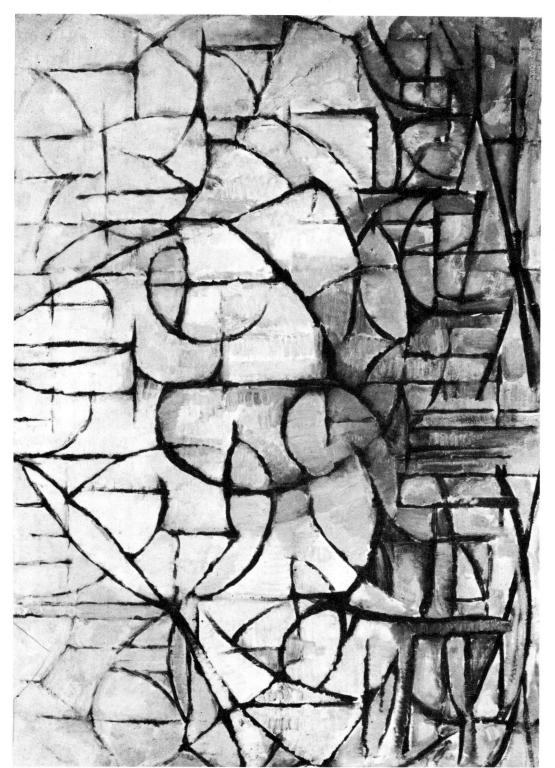

PIET MONDRIAN. *Composition 2.* 1922. 21¾ x 21″.
The Solomon R. Guggenheim Museum, New York

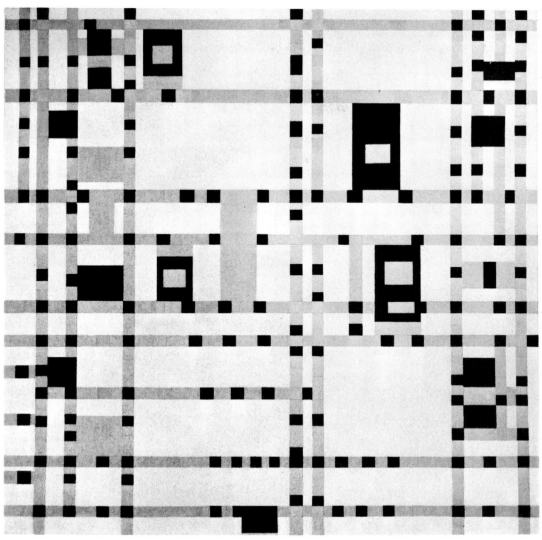

PIET MONDRIAN. *Broadway Boogie Woogie.* 1942–43. 50 x 50″.
Museum of Modern Art, New York

GIORGIO DE CHIRICO. *Melancholy and Mystery of a Street.* 1914. 33½ x 27¼".
Collection Mr. and Mrs. Stanley R. Resor, New Canaan, Connecticut.
P: MUSEUM OF MODERN ART, NEW YORK

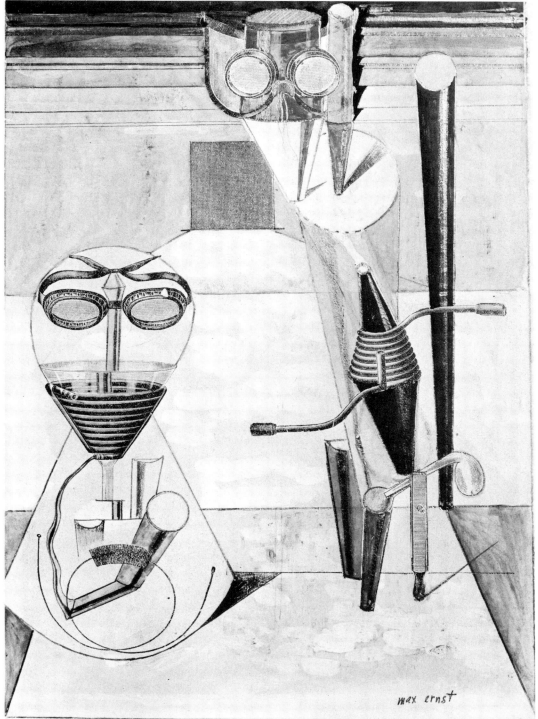

1 Kupferblech 1 zinkblech 1 gummituch 2 tastzirkel 1 abflußfernrohr 1 röhrender mensch

MAX ERNST. 1 Copper Plate 1 Zinc Plate 1 Rubber Towel 2 Calipers
1 Drainpipe Telescope 1 Roaring Man. 1920. Collage, 12 x 9″.
Collection Hans Arp, Meudon. P: MUSEUM OF MODERN ART, NEW YORK

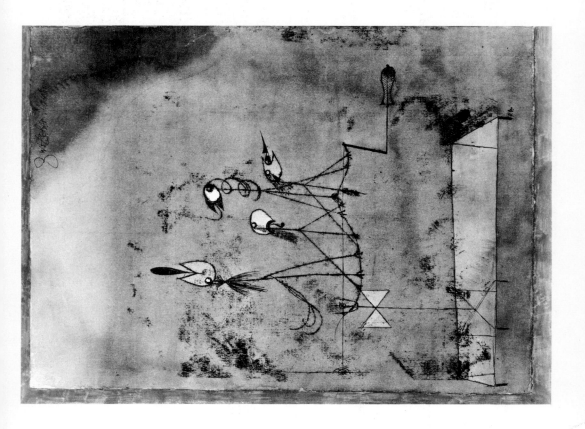

OPPOSITE PAGE, LEFT
(A) PAUL KLEE.
Twittering Machine. 1922.
Watercolor, pen, and ink, 16¼ x 12″.
Museum of Modern Art,
New York (Purchase)

OPPOSITE PAGE, RIGHT
(B) PAUL KLEE.
Park near L(ucerne).
1938. 39½ x 27½″.
Klee Foundation,
Bern, Switzerland

RIGHT
MAX ERNST. *Swamp Angel.*
1940. 26½ x 32½″.
Collection Kenneth Macpherson, Rome

OPPOSITE PAGE,
LEFT

(A) HENRI MATISSE.
The Plumed Hat.
1919. Pencil drawing,
20½ x 14″.
Collection
John S. Newberry, Jr.,
Grosse Pointe Farms,
Michigan

OPPOSITE PAGE,
RIGHT

(B) PABLO PICASSO.
Mother and Child.
1921–22. 38 x 28″.
Collection
Mr. and Mrs.
Alex L. Hillman,
New York

RIGHT

PABLO PICASSO.
Minotauromachy.
1935. Etching,
19½ x 27¼″.
Museum of Modern
Art, New York
(Purchase)

ABOVE

PABLO PICASSO. *Guernica*. 1937. 11′6″ x 25′8″.
On loan to the Museum of Modern Art, New York from the artist

OPPOSITE PAGE

BEN SHAHN. *Liberation*. 1945. 30 x 39½″.
Collection James Thrall Soby, New Canaan, Connecticut

JOAN MIRÓ. *Composition.*
1933. 51¼ x 63½".
Wadsworth Atheneum,
Hartford, Connecticut

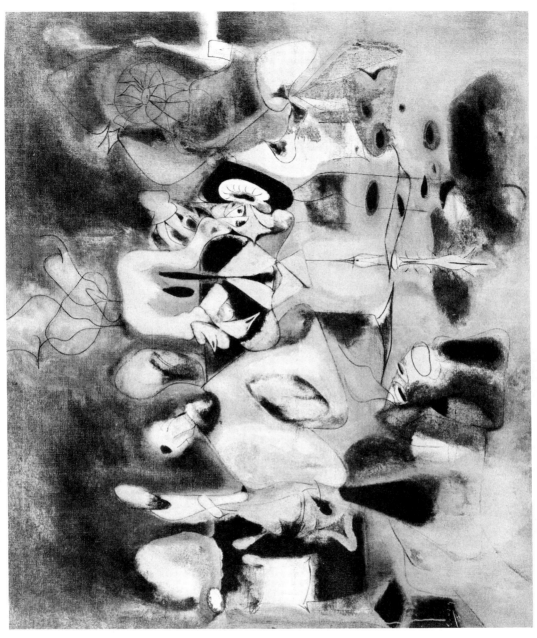

ARSHILE GORKY.
The Diary of a Seducer.
1945. 50 x 62".
Collection Mr. and Mrs. William
A. M. Burden, New York

JACKSON POLLOCK. *Number 32.* 1950. 9′ x 15′1½″. Collection Mrs. Lee Krasner Pollock, Springs, Long Island. P: HANS NAMUTH, NEW YORK

INDEX

All references are to page numbers. Names of artists are set in CAPITALS,
titles of works of art are given in *italics*.

LIST OF PHOTOGRAPHIC SOURCES

AND THEIR ABBREVIATIONS IN THE PICTURE CAPTIONS

ACL	© Archives centrales iconographiques, Brussels
ALINARI	Fratelli Alinari, Florence
AM. MUS. N.H.	American Museum of Natural History, New York
ANDERSON	Anderson, Rome
ANDREWS	Wayne Andrews, Brooklyn, New York
ARCH. PHOTO.	Archives Photographiques, Paris
BIJTEBIER	Paul Bijtebier, Brussels
BROGI	Brogi, Florence
BULLOZ	J.-E. Bulloz, Paris
COURTAULD I.	Courtauld Institute, University of London
DEPT. ARCH. INDIA	Department of Archaeology, Government of India, New Delhi
DTSCH. KUNSTVERL.	Deutscher Kunstverlag, Munich
ELISOFON	Eliot Elisofon, © Time, Inc., New York
FIORENTINI	Fiorentini, Venice
FOND. CINI	Istituto di Storia dell'Arte, Fondazione Giorgio Cini, Venice
FOT. UNIONE	Fototeca, Unione Internazionale degli Istituti . . . , Rome
FRANTZ	Alison Frantz, Athens
GAI	German Archeological Institute
GFN	Gabinetto Fotografico Nazionale, Rome
GIRAUDON	Giraudon, Paris
GROTH-KIMBALL	Irmgard Groth-Kimball, Mexico City
GUIMET	Archives Musée Guimet, Paris
HIRMER	Max Hirmer Verlag, Munich

KENNEDY	Clarence Kennedy, Northampton, Massachusetts
KERSTING	A. F. Kersting, London
INA MEXICO	Instituto Nacional de Antopología, Mexico City
MANSELL	The Mansell Collection, London
MARBURG	Foto-Marburg, Marburg/Lahn
MAS	A. y R. Mas, Barcelona
MET. MUS. N. Y.	Metropolitan Museum of Art, New York
NBR LONDON	© National Buildings Record, London
OR. INST.	Oriental Institute, University of Chicago
RCHM LONDON	Royal Commission on Historic Monuments (Crown copyright reserved)
ROUBIER	Jean Roubier, Paris
SBB	Formerly Staatliche Bildstelle, Berlin, available through Deutscher Kunstverlag, Munich
SCHMIDT-GLASSNER	Helga Schmidt-Glassner, Stuttgart
EDWIN SMITH	Edwin Smith, London
KIDDER SMITH	G. E. Kidder Smith, New York
SOPR. GALL. FLOR.	Soprintendenza alle Gallerie, Florence
STATE ADM. OF MON.	State Administration of Monuments, formerly Photometric Institute, Prague
VINCENT	John B. Vincent, Berkeley, California
VIZZAVONA	Vizzavona, Paris
WARD	Clarence Ward, Oberlin, Ohio